THE BIBLE
AND THE
LITERARY CRITIC

AMOS N. WILDER

THE BIBLE
AND THE
LITERARY CRITIC

FORTRESS PRESS   MINNEAPOLIS

THE BIBLE AND THE LITERARY CRITIC

Scripture quotations unless otherwise noted are from the Revised Standard Version of the Bible, copyright © 1946, 1952, and 1971 by the Division of Christian Education of the National Council of Churches.

Cover design: Pollock Design Group
Interior design: Publishers' WorkGroup

Library of Congress Cataloging-in-Publication Data

The Bible and the literary critic / Amos N. Wilder.
    p. cm.
  Includes bibliographical references and index.
  ISBN 0-8006-2436-X (alk. paper)
    1. Bible as literature.   2. Literature—Philosophy.   3. Bible—
Hermeneutics.   4. Bible—Criticism, interpretation, etc.   5. Bible.
N.T.—Criticism, interpretation, etc.—History—20th century.
6. Wilder, Amos Niven, 1895-   .   I. Wilder, Amos Niven, 1895-
BS535.B485   1990
220.6'6—dc20   90–49740
                                                              CIP

The paper used in this publication meets the minimum requirements of American National Standard for Information Science—Permanence of Paper for Printed Library Materials, ANSI Z329.48-1984.   ∞™

Manufactured in the U.S.A.   AF 1–2436

95   94   93   92   91   1   2   3   4   5   6   7   8   9   10

To the two Catharines,
Mother and Daughter

Contents

PART THREE
GENRES, RHETORICS AND MEANING

Preface

In speaking in this volume of literary criticism I have in mind the current explorations which are proving so illuminating in our humanistic disciplines in general. There is no reason why these probes and methods may not profitably be directed to the Scriptures.

This whole activity, of course, is highly diverse, arising as it has out of various new insights into language and human discourse. Thus we are confronted with a fertile debate about approaches to literature and one to which biblical studies may well make a significant contribution.

This development has moved beyond familiar views of literary criticism. In that tradition the category of "literary" was associated with aesthetic and rhetorical aspects of literature. Prominence was assigned to matters of style, eloquence, lyricism, virtuosity, if also to humanistic sensibilities. In consideration of the Bible, this meant selective appreciation of passages deemed sublime or masterpieces.

This Romantic approach had its inevitable corollary in the deserved but misconceived appreciation of the King James translation. To put it perhaps hyperbolically, there were those who swooned at the cadences of the Authorized Version but often had no understanding of or even concern with the meaning of the writings. For a proper recognition of the superlative features of this rendering readers should know more about the scholarly and literary labors which went into its achievement. The Elizabethan scholar Ward Allen, of Auburn University, was the first to discover and publish actual worksheets of the King's revisers: *Translating for King James* (1969), and *Translating the New Testament Epistles, 1604–1611* (1977). These specimens exhibit the numerous options offered by earlier translators and the resources of the living speech of the period. But they also show a masterly grasp of the Greek originals whose usage and purport the translators likewise weigh in their final renderings.

That older approach to the arts of literature which I have identified should be respected, but its appreciations should be carried over into a less subjective critique. The category of literary and the task of literary criticism properly go deeper. If literature is the register of cultural and human realities we are directed to an inquisition into all the operations of the word and the factors which underlie our various rhetorics. Literary criticism today is thus called to this more searching study of our texts. As applied to the Bible this thrust should not be misunderstood. It does not represent a merely superficial study of the aesthetics of the canon. Nor should it be disparaged as oblivious of other types of criticism and interpretation. Since we have to do with literary texts any light which can be thrown on the modes and functioning of their rhetoric has a bearing on all such investigations.

For the purpose of illustration I trust that I shall be excused if I adduce three experiences of my own which helped clarify for me the role of literary criticism in the study of the Bible.

The first had to do with the power of myth, in this case the eschatological myth in our early Christian texts. This goes back to the early twenties when scholars generally read the apocalyptic visions in literalist terms. The impact of Albert Schweitzer's *Quest* was important for me, but even he had a basically literalist interpretation of Jesus' outlook on the future. It was in fact my experience in World War I which uncovered for me the true dynamics of the language. There the successive passions of ordeal, utopian hopes, disenchantment and modulated expectation illuminated the evangelical drama, and the feature of the imminence of the goal in view was an essential part of the outlook. To recognize this kind of mentality and ideation in the background of our Gospels has further corollaries and involves many cultural and interdisciplinary perceptions. This example serves for me as a testimony to the enrichment of our methods which a literary criticism can contribute. Surely the operations of the mythic imagination fall within its scope.

My second example has to do with the power of metaphor. Even after the time of C.H. Dodd and Joachim Jeremias the parables of Jesus were still widely seen as illustrations, concessions to a popular audience, epitomies or allegories. They were analogies or figures for the purpose of public debate. Under the influence of the New Criticism they could be seen as rhetorical tropes or even as autonomous icons.

I well remember the early days of the Parables Seminar of the Society of Biblical Literature. In the late sixties and early seventies, such colleagues as Robert Funk, Dan Via, Dominic Crossan, James Robinson, Robert Tannehill and William Beardslee engaged in vigorous debate about this aspect of Jesus' teaching. Seeing the parables as action-metaphors, we had been impressed by views of metaphor held by literary critics, especially Ezra Pound. This stressed the radical shift of vision characterizing this poetic vehicle. In consequence we saw Jesus' parables not as illustrations which could have a discursive interpretation but as revelatory, as epiphanic. They opened up a new reality. This illumination was not only projected but like a spell captured the hearer and invaded his outlook.

This development is again a testimony to the contributions of literary criticism. It is also worth noting that the activity of the Parables Seminar led to the founding in 1973 of *Semeia,* whose first issues were devoted to the parables. This journal opened up contacts for biblical scholars with workers in linguistics, structuralism and other disciplines.

A third area involving literary criticism and one on which no other biblical approach had really enlightened me was narrativity. Of course we had all known about the large place that stories, myths, saga and recital have in the Scriptures. Historical criticism recognized the antecedents of the biblical myths and fables in the ancient Orient and could make comparisons, chiefly thematic and theological. Motifs of Hellenistic romance were recognized in the Gospels and the Acts of the Apostles. But all this went only halfway. Why narrative in the first place? What differing assumptions determined different kinds of storying and plotting? Erich Auerbach's contribution only opened the way to this kind of literary inquiry.

Rhetorics reflect not only particular cultural contexts but ontological presuppositions. Differing views of such basic categories as time, space and causation inevitably shape the arts of a tribe or society, not least those of communication. The way stories are told is an immediate reflex of their either firm or tenuous grasp on experience; their static, cyclical or directional experience of succession; their sense of human agency as it appears in their fabulation.

This kind of rhetorical discrimination is particularly revealing when applied to the Scriptures. It is not only the prominence of narrative which characterizes the biblical word but the controlling teleology of its *epos* and the responsible role of the human participants in the portrayal. These features go back to an a priori anthropology very different from that which governs the fabulations of Homer or of India. The basic category of subjectivity or identity and its agency is overshadowed in them by Fate and Fortuna, by the caprices of the gods or the sway of impersonal realities.

Here again the fictive world of Jesus' narrative parables is instructive. Here we have sharply focused individuals acting and reacting in a variety of quotidian situations. Whether knaves, weaklings or faithful, their choices are woven fatefully into the web of common human experience, and this realism extends in the future perspective to an outcome represented variously as harvest, day of reckoning or banquet. This aspect of the worldliness of Jesus' parables has been persuasively analyzed in James Breech's *The Silence of Jesus* (1983).

Prior, therefore, to any thematic considerations with respect to these stories we should attend to what we must call their ontology, their vision of existence. This is one which prolongs the covenant conception of Israel so deeply linked with the creaturely, somatic, economic and historical life of humankind. These ultimate premises shape the scenarios of the parables and the evangelical history generally. The story-world differs from that of other recitals dictated by a more tenuous and unstable sense of the self and the time-process. Again, rhetorics, speech modes, reflect ontological assumptions. Literary and rhetorical criticism cannot stop short of these discriminations.

These three examples of the agenda of literary criticism as it bears on the Scriptures seem to me to warrant the task. It is all the more overdue since the biblical writings have largely lain outside the purview of our humanistic disciplines. The traditional scope of literary criticism has been understandably oriented to aesthetic and inter-textual aspects of letters, to rhetorics in a conventional sense, together with a rich sensitivity to cultural and human values. Yet this exclusion of the deeper ramifications of significance in our writings has of late begun to trouble our specialists and teachers. We are more aware today of the labyrinths of meaning which underlie our texts. These send those specialists and teachers in pursuit of far-ranging cultural factors but also of motivations which they have been reluctant to address.

It is at this point that the Bible and its legacies become an issue. It is true that the biblical and theological components in our Western writings have compelled attention. But academic study of such writers as Dante, Milton, Pascal and Jonathan Edwards has never been at ease. It has had to restrict itself to what it sees as properly literary assessment without exploring the biblical premises of the writings. This restraint has operated in dealing with the Bible itself.

Today, however, when literature is seen not as belles lettres but as text, and the Bible not as canon but similarly as text, the latter is open to new queries, both linguistic and rhetorical. These relate to the general phenomenology of discourse with the result that the rhetorics of the Bible can be explored and compared at this level with those of other texts, whether stories, oracles, hymns or litanies.

My studies in this book are directed toward this new front in the literary study of the Bible. I first explore contemporary literary criticism and its premises (chapters 1–3). I then sketch in the background through my long personal recall of the vicissitudes of modern New Testament scholarship from Albert Schweitzer to Norman Perrin (chapters 4–6). Finally, I devote several studies to narrativity and to the issues raised by what is called post-modernism. I also find it relevant to consider the bearings of the literary criticism of the Scriptures on the wider task of the theological appraisal of literature generally. In this connection I seize the opportunity to pay tribute to Nathan A. Scott, Jr., as he nears retirement, for his extensive contributions in this area and his friendship through many years in common pursuits.

In concluding this Preface I wish to register my appreciation of the many workers, both theological and lay, who have contributed to

PART ONE

NEW SOUNDINGS

1

George Steiner and
The Literary Guide
to the Bible

In reviewing Frank Kermode's book, *The Genesis of Secrecy,* I observe that the canonical texts might well blunt the tools of the literary critic. But I conclude that whatever his own premises might be Kermode has served all of us in opening up "the depths of the world" in Mark's narrative.

I found myself somewhat torn the year following Kermode's Norton Lectures when Helen Gardner pressed me about them, since she devoted one of her own lectures to disagreement with him. She likewise had written on Scripture, and as a churchwoman with some initiation in biblical criticism she felt that Kermode had been too skeptical about the sources and had erred in matters of biblical allegory.

This project has interested me since I first heard of it from Frank Kermode several years ago. He wrote me that he was then thinking of a series of volumes, each on some book of the Bible, and was exploring suggestions as to contributors. He hinted at my being involved, and I demurred for reasons of age. We had become acquainted in 1969 at the Round Hill conference on religion and literature. I was in touch with him again when he gave his Norton Lectures at Harvard on Mark's Gospel, in 1977 and 1978. —A.N.W.

The Literary Guide to the Bible, edited by Robert Alter and Frank Kermode, was published in 1987 by the Harvard University Press. George Steiner's review was published in *The New Yorker,* January 11, 1988. This essay appeared originally as "The Literary Critic and the Bible: George Steiner on *The Literary Guide to the Bible*" in the journal *Religion and Intellectual Life* 6 (Spring/Summer 1989), published by the Association for Religion and Intellectual Life, College of New Rochelle, New Rochelle, New York.

In any case, the issues raised then as in the Alter/Kermode *Guide* (not to mention Northrop Frye's *The Great Code: The Bible and Literature* [1982]) strike home to all of us concerned with biblical studies and especially to those of us who have now for some time wished to apply the skills and codes of secular literary criticism to the Scriptures. In bringing "literary criticism" (and "rhetorical criticism") to bear on the Scriptures we are confronted with various traditional and professional views of literary study and its scope (note Helen Gardner's earlier title, "The Limits of Criticism"). But there was also the problem of the particularity of the biblical texts. Is literary criticism to be identified mainly with aesthetic categories? If it merges with linguistic and therefore with epistemological and ultimately with ontological criteria, where does any distinction arise in comparative and world literature as regards sacred books and the biblical canon?

Much of our pioneering as biblical interpreters in appropriating the strategies of the New Criticism or of narratology or the study of genres has stayed within the limits of a humanistic approach as familiar in comparative literature. Even structuralist and sociological analyses or concerns with orality can be pursued as objective and descriptive apart from ultimate issues of revelation and commitment. In the case of Northrop Frye we can recognize a massive instance of our inherited inclination to set off the literary approach from supposedly nonliterary considerations in the texts, including the biblical. Such other dimensions of whatever writings or classics—the social, the historical or the theological—are not denied, but they are bracketed out for other investigators and interpreters.

The fact is, however, that literary criticism generally has varied widely in theory and practice with respect to its proper boundaries. Classic concern with the aesthetic order has directed main attention to works, the aesthetic or literary object, to forms, styles and media, through their changing schools and legacies. Behind this demarcation, in art, letters and criticism, lay various philosophical premises, Platonic, Aristotelian, idealist or Romantic, which structured the distinctions.

But the deeper human context of literature and the resonance of its arts have always drawn even academic criticism into more problematic areas of meaning and assessment. In the literature of the Romantic movement the boundaries between art and prophecy were breached, and in the case of Matthew Arnold we can see this widening of the critical tradition extending to the rhetorics of the Bible. For our later period we can recognize this dilemma of the critical tradition in T.S. Eliot's wrestling both to continue it and to absorb new refractory data into it.

I sketch in this retrospect as a background to the topic indicated in my title. In reviewing the Alter/Kermode *Literary Guide to the Bible* in *The New Yorker* (January 11, 1988) George Steiner is very severe on the premises and contents of this ambitious undertaking. The main issue here, it seems to me, arises precisely at the point I have been making. What is literary criticism? What are its limits? In view of the flexibility of its definition and agenda in our period widely different criteria of its practice can lead to the kind of disagreement reflected in this instance.

No doubt Steiner is right in evoking distinctive and transcending features of the biblical texts which he misses in the literary treatments provided here of the sacred writings. Where is the *mysterium tremendum* and the terror of the divine encounter? Steiner finds that in this literary-critical approach "a terrible blandness is born," resulting in a sense of the Scripture "cocooned in academic poise and urbanity."

In the history of scholarly labors on the Bible Steiner observes an astonishing reversal. The ancient arts of commentary which have come down to us through patristic, Talmudic, medieval and Renaissance scholiasts and glossators, all of which were devoted to the texts in their integrity and authority, have suffered a fateful truncation in our rationalistic epoch. But today literary criticism, recognizing the impoverishment of those ancient methods, has sought, as in the case of Matthew Arnold, to reclaim that total approach. But, says Steiner, "this will not work." This method, this *instrumentum*, is too circumscribed to engage with the transcending sublimity of the writings.

There are two dimensions of the Scripture which Steiner identifies as beyond the reach of literary criticism as currently practiced: its "particularity" (by comparison even with such works as Shakespeare's *Lear*) and its "provocations," or "summons" to human response. On this latter point we are reminded of Northrop Frye's distinction: The Bible is literature but differs in its aspect of *kerygma*. The question is whether this massive and searching provocation of our human disposition and inertia can be registered in any literary appraisal.

Steiner prefaces his strictures on the *Guide* with highly appreciative comments on many of the contributions in the volume. These authors bring highly sophisticated skills in all aspects of literary and linguistic assessment to the various books of the canon, with extensive illumination of their rhetorics and structures. So dominant is this feature that Steiner sees the volume as written especially for those who are conversant with contemporary investigation, literary structuralism, poetics and narratology. But then he turns to his weighty reservations.

It is important to note that Steiner is not setting the limitations of a literary approach over against that of faith. It is at this point that it is useful to compare Donald Davie's detailed review of the *Guide* in *The New Republic* (October 26, 1987). Davie also praises the expertise of many of the contributors. But as a committed Anglican he is somewhat nervous about those points where the literary strategies tend to obscure the devotional dimension and the witness of the sacred writings. If for Steiner the literary-critical scrutiny scants the depth and power of such books as Job, Davie argues with the historical premises of Edmund Leech and with Gabriel Josipovici's deprecation of the ritual drama of the faith as "thinned" out (appealing to Mary Douglas) in the Epistle to the Hebrews. Indeed, Davie closes with a direct challenge to Kermode himself with respect to the latter's presentation of the overall masterly "contrivance" and manipulation of effects which characterize the work of the author of the Gospel of John. He sees this as no less than an invitation to disbelief.

The quandaries as to the proper scope of a literary criticism of the Bible are well indicated by these two critiques. As a rationale for our *Literary Guide* we may cite the words of one of its editors, Robert Alter, in his "Introduction to the Old Testament":

> According to one common line of thought, the Hebrew Bible exhibits certain literary embellishments and literary interludes, but those who would present "the Bible as literature" must turn it around to an odd angle from its own original emphases, which are theological, legislative, historiographic and moral. This opposition between literature and the really serious things collapses the moment we realize that it is the exception in any culture for literary invention to be a purely aesthetic activity.

This generous charter evidently opens the scope of literary appraisal, but Steiner and Davie are both highly dissatisfied with the outcome.

In view of their strictures I myself feel marginally on the defensive since I wrote such an appreciative comment for the jacket of the volume. As a biblical scholar long wistful not only for closer dialogue between theologians and the arts but for disciplined literary illumination of the Scriptures, I hailed this long-overdue engagement of so many specialists from outside the theological guild with the biblical texts:

> I am enthusiastic about this volume, which is a veritable thesaurus of literary and human evaluation of the Scriptures, both absorbing and authoritative. It is as though someone had pushed back a lot of shutters and opened windows in an ancient library long obscured by stained glass and cobwebs. I expect that many will be induced by it to go back to reading the Bible after a long lapse.

Like any brief characterization my encomium did not take account of unevennesses in the treatments of the various books and topics nor of debatable angles of approach. I was pleased first of all by the unprecedented project itself, that so many humanistically oriented and "secular" specialists should have crossed the great divide which has so long sequestered the Jewish and Christian classics. I was also happy that this kind of attention should have been given to the Bible for a public largely illiterate in this ancient library or knowing of it only as the enclave of a devout tradition, the stellar labors on which by modern scholars and interpreters remain unknown or baffling to them.

In this situation, both as regards our modern readership and as regards the situation in biblical studies, it is highly opportune that so many collaborators versed in interdisciplinary studies should assess the biblical texts through their differing lenses. The literary-critical approach is flexible enough to encourage various kinds of probings in the literature and illumination of various facets and levels of the particular writings. Whatever greater or ultimate import the Bible may have, it is made up of writings and therefore at that level calls for whatever light from whatever quarter we may bring on human discourse and communication.

But this brings me back to George Steiner's ostensibly unarguable objections. There are registers of awe, terror and apocalyptic drama in the Scriptures which an urbane and academic book like this fails to signal. Indeed, these heights and depths of the Bible transcend the reach and modalities of literary criticism. I am paraphrasing his observations, but one can see why he is led to the conclusion that this whole approach "will not work." I note again that he is not demurring on dogmatic grounds, as sometimes appears in Donald Davie's review. It is a question of the parameters of the imagination and their evocation in the Bible which elude the rhetorical procedures and calipers whether of historical or literary criticism.

In reply to this, no doubt the editors and contributors of the volume would plead that their literary approach is to be viewed as exploratory and penultimate. They could appeal to the main tradition of literary criticism which like the older category of "rhetoric" has accepted a delimitation of its domain, satisfied that its regional illumination might serve wider inquiries and more ultimate appraisals. After all, Alter and Kermode affix a relatively modest title to their compilation: "A Literary Guide to the Study of the Bible."

But more needs to be said here. The main point to be made in reply to Steiner is that those dimensions of the Bible which he identifies as transcending *need themselves to be clarified* and their rhetorics not tamed but related to all that we can learn about the imagination and its operations from whatever disciplines and circumspections. The import of the most stunning epiphanies and prodigies in Scripture, and of its unfathomable voices, dialogues, transactions and words of the wise, these unwonted ranges of discourse, is surely not to be "controlled" by our categories but brought within reach of our screens of response and our discrimination. Granted that our methods as practiced in the *Guide* fall short of the task, their further refinement and enrichment offer the best promise of an appropriate reading of the texts. If modern literary criticism, richly orchestrated by inclusion of linguistic, cultural and philosophical criteria, has gone so far in appreciation of the depth of our literary classics there is no reason why the same widening scrutiny may not move revealingly toward illumination of our biblical charters.

By limiting the scope of literary criticism and reneging on this large task Steiner intends to exalt the "particularity" of the Scriptures. The numinous and the sublime repel the dwarfed exercises of our grammarians and rhetoricians. But this leaves him in the position of those who romantically or mystically acclaim sheer transcendence without any structure or rationale for identifying its character and relevancies.

This kind of uninstructed and unstructured reading of the divine-human wrestling in the Bible can lead to highly arbitrary interpretation of particular texts. Steiner's well-known and admirable concern with the Holocaust, and with anti-Semitism, leads him into a mis-reading of Paul's discussion of Israel in his Epistle to the Romans, which a situated rhetorical criticism would have obviated.

Referring to "ugly issues" which are skirted in the *Guide* Steiner writes as follows:

> The all too precise prefiguring of Christ's role and agony in the Psalms, in Deutero-Isaiah, is only glancingly referred to. This, in turn, makes it hardly possible for the modern reader to apprehend the bitter, wholly consequent hatred of the Jews expressed in Romans—a hatred incomparably phrased, metaphorized by Paul, and, one cannot but feel, bearing its death fruit in our century. It is just because the Psalms and the literature of prophecy in the Old Testament foretell Jesus so graphically that the rejection of Jesus by the Jews of his own day strikes Paul as a specifically suicidal blasphemy, as an act of self-negation which sets mankind on the treadmill of its imprisonment in history.

As a matter of fact, if there is anywhere in the New Testament where the "irrepressible conflict" between Israel and the church is lifted above anger and bitterness it is precisely in this letter of Paul. As far as his personal attitude to his fellow Israelites was in question, Paul would have wished to be "accursed from Christ for my brethren, my kinsmen according to the flesh." In speaking of God's providential dealing with Israel and the Gentiles he recognizes the operations of both "goodness and severity," mercy and judgment. Under the head of severity to Israel he writes not of "anger" (lower case) in the relationships of "history" (lower case) but of the impersonal "Wrath" (upper case) or enchainment of God's World-Historical (upper case) decrees looking toward eventual reconciliation and universal salvation. To see any incitement to hatred in this philosophy of history would be like interpreting Abraham Lincoln's theme of the Lord's righteous judgments in his Second Inaugural as a call to embitterment.

The fateful and entangled issue Paul was dealing with in Romans required the kind of survey Paul gives it. Steiner appears to think that this painful history should have been skirted or innocuously simplified. Any good commentary on Romans could have clarified for him Paul's categories and argument. But this is a case where his play with wide-ranging intertextual motifs and his use of metaphor call for a literary and sociocultural assessment for any more adequate reading.

No doubt the current stage of this approach as applied to the Bible leaves much out of account. Hence Steiner's dissatisfaction. But the method itself should not be put out of court. If the literary analysis, also as a secular project, is widened as it should be to include all that pertains to language—and therefore to the whole range of significations not only aesthetic but sociocultural, attitudinal, moral and ontological—and if these circumspections are built on and interwoven with the insights already so epochally achieved by historical criticism, then indeed the way is open for a new postdogmatic appropriation of our biblical classics and heritage. Advances in this direction have already been made in the biblical guild itself.

I conclude with one further instance of the biblical portrayal which Steiner very plausibly sets apart from the compass of the literary critic. The accounts in our Gospels of the Passion of Christ and the crucifixion in their tenor and with their shuddering cosmic repercussions would seem evidently to baffle any such "wisdom of the world" as might be invoked in the strategies of our critics. This kind of transaction relates to a different order or galaxy of understanding than those of even our greatest literary classics. But this exclusion suggests a kind of docetism which contradicts the whole character of the biblical story. It fits with the idea of a God who is only a cipher of transcendence and who in his ways has not let himself be known.

In his account of the death of Christ Matthew concludes:

> And, behold, the veil of the temple was rent in twain from the top to the bottom; and the earth did quake, and the rocks rent; And the graves were opened; and many bodies of the saints which slept arose, And came out of the graves after his resurrection, and went into the holy city, and appeared unto many. (27:51-53, KJV)

Here the stupor of the event and its dissolution of all our coordinates of space, and time and space, are conveyed by both apocalyptic and theocratic motifs. This mytho-logical narration bridges the diurnal and the eternal, nature and the preternatural, past, present and future, and life and death by a dramatization which, again, solicits all the modalities of literary/rhetorical study. As in Job or John's Apocalypse or *The Divine Comedy* we find ourselves in an uncanny theater or echo chamber where ultimate agencies and designs are glimpsed, as in Dante's *alta fantasia*.

There is surely no impropriety, let alone sacrilege, in our literary soundings here, any more than in such probings of the stupendous theophany of Vishnu in the *Bhagavad-Gita*. I have elsewhere called attention to an analogy of this procedure in T.S. Eliot's discussion, in his essay on Dante, of *La Vita Nuova*. Here, as Eliot observes, the poet's first youthful encounter with Beatrice and its affective sequel are clothed in a nimbus of the symbol and figuration of his school and time. For us to know what really happened in all its purport we must initiate ourselves in the language Dante employed with all its categories and implications.

The limitations of the literary critic in all such high endeavors are only partly due to the rarefied sublimity of such texts. They call for imaginative endowment in the critic, and many of our scholars and specialists, whatever their other expertise, lack such poetic or visionary talent. They can therefore only go halfway in retracing the operations which enter into the composition and crystallization of such discourse as that with which we are here concerned.

With respect to all such writings whose theater, gamut and idiom so baffle our usual codes, special antennae are called for. Our best humanistic discriminations need to be opened up to a richer apperceptive register. But any such more adequate screening of the biblical rhetorics by our literary specialists will no doubt run parallel with the hermeneutical ventures of the theologians over much of the course, with each approach instructing the other.

2

The Literary Critic
and the New Testament:
Frank Kermode on the
Gospel of Mark

PREMISES

Frank Kermode's book, *The Genesis of Secrecy: On the Interpretation of Narrative,* will no doubt be seen as a breakthrough on the part of the professional literary critic in dealing with the Scriptures. Coming so close to Northrop Frye's volume *The Great Code: The Bible and Literature* (1982, 1981), these Norton Lectures at Harvard (1977–78, published in 1979) represent a searching probe of probably the oldest and most crucial New Testament Gospel. Here whatever illuminations of the canonical texts may be forthcoming, so also dissonances of method and text should be exposed, looking no doubt toward a further refinement of method.

In this treatment of Mark's narrative, including that author's view of the parables, Kermode understandably makes much of the enigmatic in the writing and associates this with the indeterminacy of all narrative and the "unfollowable" character of all recitals and, indeed,

This return to Frank Kermode's notable book takes the form not of a consecutive review but of a series of probings and notes on the task itself. This unwonted incursion of secular criticism into Holy Writ raises far-reaching questions not only about narrative but also about the sacred text and critical method today. If Scripture here is illuminated it also provides a new and unsettling test for current critical premises and strategies. This confrontation must be pursued, and Kermode has opened up the issues in a masterly way. If my reflections are seen as just another example of de Man's "resistance to theory," I trust that they are sufficiently grounded to avert the usual charge of conformity to accepted ideas and ideological defensiveness. In any case, I continue very grateful to Frank Kermode for his many courtesies and for setting up the absorbing issues which I here try to deal with.—A.N.W.

of the world itself. In the course of this inquisition, which appears to be supported by Mark's own thematic and lack of closure, Kermode comes up with what he calls a "cheerless" view of our human situation. At most he identifies, on an analogy with Kafka's parable of the Gatekeeper of the Law, "intermittent radiances" issuing from the impasses of experience reflected in the occult structures of Mark's composition.

In an early review of the book I expressed appreciation of this more sobering assessment of Mark contributed by an undomesticated reading. Kermode has drawn our attention to the way in which "the depths of the world" are exposed in this Gospel. This could serve as a salutary foil to any facile view of the salvation announced in the Gospel and of its costs. I still think that as with the work of such modern writers as Samuel Beckett this kind of rebuke to indurated assumptions and mental habits is of first importance.

But I now think that there are aspects of Kermode's critical method which may be queried. Our author, for one thing, understandably observes that matters of faith and commitment are "not in his brief." But if it is a question of any such ontological neutrality one may well ask whether or not some similarly prior orientation in our age of suspicion may not operate here. I have in mind that widespread reaction in our age to the dogmatic layers of tradition which issues in a stance favoring the indeterminate, the undecidable and the open. In the light of this stance, Kermode can, as it seems to me, misread the affirmation which runs through Mark's Gospel despite its negativities.

Another questionable investment behind Kermode's practice is today even more fateful. It bears especially on current views of narrativity. This author appears to hold that since all narrative is open to interpretation and reinterpretation no particular reading of a recital can be favored, let alone as normative. It is true that ultimate mystery circumscribes all human reporting. But surely there are considerations bearing on the intent of the reporter and the data that he or she structures which argue for one meaning rather than another. We are not speaking of stories which are deliberate mystifications.

This degree of confidence in a narrator today encounters a veto from another widespread critical persuasion. Granted the intention of the narrator to tell his own story, he is not the master of his tale. So massive are the anterior compulsions of apperception and imagination in his medium of language that his account and his scenarios are infiltrated by distorting legacies. In Kermode's reading of Mark one can recognize this kind of qualification of the Gospel history as one aspect of that enigmatic view of it presented by this critic. The propriety of these readings needs to be probed in particular passages, but one need not conclude that Mark's narrative dissolves in enigma without intended purport.

In this preliminary query as to Kermode's critical premises we must note finally that difficult *topos* so mooted in recent criticism identified with text and textuality. Here, too, our author shows his openness to the view, maintained with many nuances and ambiguities, that "there is nothing outside the text." The text, recognizing its intertextuality, is its own world and is not transparent upon some ulterior reality involving referentiality and correspondence. The force of this view derives from a persuasive sense of the definitive role of language in establishing our human reality.

With this view of a text, however, one can see how a narrative like one of our Gospels can be construed as fabulation rather than history in any sense. The course of the recital is dictated by intratextual and anterior motifs, and any constraints on or import into its meaning afforded by historical or cultural assessment are derogated. In any case, these preoccupations of contemporary critical method, with whatever insights and limitations, evidently weigh with Frank Kermode as he addresses his biblical text.

THE LURE OF INTERPRETATION:
HERMES AS SLEUTH

The professional biblical scholar will not look on this foray into his field by an Elizabethan specialist as an intrusion. But he or she has had experience of fumbling and extravagant "readings" of the Bible by amateurs and those with supposedly special insights—such as lawyers who think they can explain the trial of Jesus. Professionals, therefore, look with some skepticism on such a venture as this. We wonder if the new tools of the critic may not be blunted by such exceptional works as those of the canon. Even though admirers of such masters as Kermode, we may be wary in our domain of such Greeks bringing gifts. But in the present case many of our hesitancies are disarmed. Kermode is exploring the workings of narration and has no ostensible axe to grind.

The author, we may say, is interested in various fundamental "drives" in storytelling. It may be that "sense of an ending" which seems to be such a universal operator in fabulation. Or, as in the present case, it may be the lure of some deeper sense in a recital. Stories, like the world itself, seem to call for interpretation, for decoding. There is some greater truth or reality, some secret, out there behind them. An allegory is only a very simple example of this kind of overlaying of the sense. Thus Kermode is primarily concerned here with that universal "motor" and appeal of narrative which, as both pregnant with meaning and often baffling, challenges the hearer or reader.

If the world and stories about it have this puzzling appeal it can take many forms. It is perhaps a little strange that our author captions his book, "the genesis of *secrecy.*" But it is true that particular hidden meanings can be looked on as privileged and so can become exclusionary and forbidden. So we get "insiders" and "outsiders." Kermode is here no doubt interested in the role played by authority and institutions in fixing the true sense of tradition. This would chime with another of his main recurrent concerns, that with "canon" (or the category of the "classic") and the factors in canonization in literature and the arts. In the light of these interests it is not surprising that the author's attention is here turned to the Gospel of Mark in which as compared with the other Gospels riddling questions of interpretation both as to the parables and as to the hidden revelation of Jesus' ministry so come to the fore.

PRECURSORS

To situate current approaches of the literary critic to the Bible one can well look at the issues of this frontier in a wider context. The secularization of the West has moved apace since Matthew Arnold's wish to deal with the prophets and the Bible generally as he would deal with any other book or classic. His project was framed by critical and cultural premises which have since been buried by layers of new sophistications. (Yet with all his moral sentiment and urbanity Arnold has something to teach and to scandalize our modern relativists: namely, his recognition of the authority of Israel's *episteme* and his appeal to "Jacob I have loved, and Esau I have hated"!)

Going back farther, secularization was already advanced in the way in which William Blake dealt with the Bible. Yet this nondog-

matic view of the sacred texts as oracles has long since been disallowed together with other Romantic idioms of that epoch. (Yet
Blake highlighted "political" bearings of the texts, requiring some
recognition of their mimetic character.)

A major earlier option in our secularizing period for dealing with
the Bible is afforded by no less a figure than that of Hegel. It so
happens also that no less a figure than Jacques Derrida has recently
canvassed Hegel's procedures exhaustively in *Glas* (1981). No doubt
later explorers like Kermode have been warned by Hegel's massive
venture to shun any suspicion of ideology or system. Hegel reads the
canon through such lenses of his period as Reason and Freedom and
ends up by identifying the biblical Word with infinite Spirit, and
philosophy itself with Christianity. The telltale blindness of his Age
of Enlightenment and Sentiment appears in his scandalous misrepre-
sentation of the Old Testament and his anti-Semitism which Derrida
ruthlessly exposes.

In our own century the inclination to deal with the Bible as with
any other book has had its vicissitudes. The Bible has been brought
into the field of comparative literature and its attention to non-West-
ern writings. But it has also inevitably been linked with controversial
issues in the literary criticism of such works as *The Divine Comedy*.
In his *Cantos* Ezra Pound could evoke Dante's Christian epic, but his
view of Israel's sacred histories prolongs Hegel's revulsion. On the
other hand such commitments of T.S. Eliot as appear in his essay on
Dante and in those testimonies of his "retreat" disciplines echoed in
Four Quartets point indirectly to encounter with the Scriptures in his
own modern context.

Neither did Auden bring his extensive critical competence to bear
on the Bible directly, but in his *Christmas Oratorio* and in two of his
essays in *The Dyer's Hand* ("Genius and Apostle" and "Postscript:
Christianity and Art") he indicated that for him the Scriptures still
spoke with a unique voice and authority in our secularized situation.
One might venture that Auden's today altogether nonnegotiable
schema of natural and supernatural represented for him a kind of
hyperbolic version of that revelatory medium, the *epiphany,* which is
today more current.

I have referred to Northrop Frye's inestimable contribution in our
area of biblical rhetorics. That the Bible can be read like any other

book appears here to have two corollaries. Its art can be freely and exhaustively inventoried both intratextually and intertextually. But this aesthetic and rhetorical monitoring can be pursued with questions of historical and social context left in the background, and with them normative and theological issues. But however it may be with "any other book," Frye's encyclopedia of motifs of the Bible can only serve as the vestibule of a full reading. The aesthetic on which it is based will not satisfy even today's post-modernists.

Among other recent options in the critic's encounter with Scripture we should include the name of Helen Gardner. In her fence-crossing book, *The Business of Criticism* (1959), she noted among other things that in both biblical and English studies the same critical ploys were in evidence. Her example (citing Austin Farrer's diagramming of Mark's composition) was the then fashion of image monitoring in various works, much overworked. Another sign of the times was I.A. Richards's *Beyond* (1974). Here was a bold venture to confront Hellenic and Hebraic legacies, dealing with Homer and Greek tragedy on the one hand and with Job and Isaiah on the other, and including Dante in the purview. Here a kind of uncommitted structuralism identifies similar polarities in both heritages. Yet Richards cannot, like some of our linguistically oriented critics, be satisfied with a textual, nonideological scrutiny. The heirs of our Western iconoclasm resent the incubus of Israel's law and covenant, and so this critic cannot but disallow the moral and penal motifs which shaped *The Divine Comedy*.

The foregoing review will have suggested the changing aspects in the critic's approach to the Bible. But to this must now be added that more radical shift of critical premises which I identified as Kermode's "investments" in his approach to his task. Here the movement of secularization has gone farther and for many has subverted the terms of those earlier engagements with Holy Writ.

THE NORTON LECTURES

When the first of these Norton Lectures was under way at Harvard in the fall of 1977 the auditors soon realized that something extraordinary was going on. The announced title of the lectures had indicated that Professor Kermode would be directing his attention to that area currently interesting literary critics, namely, the phenomenology of narrative and especially of the novel. At least the recent tradition of the Norton Lectures, represented by a poet like Guillén and a musician like Leonard Bernstein, hardly prepared us for the subject matter addressed in this series. Perhaps, however, the theme and the scope of the lectures of his immediate predecessor, Northrop Frye, entitled *The Secular Scripture,* represented some kind of bridge to what Kermode was about. These lectures, while they did not deal directly with the biblical writings, canvassed the labyrinthine ways in which their motifs, plots and roles found analogies and echoes in our general literary heritage. Indeed, one can say that this nondogmatic survey of the intertextual ramifications of the canon, directed to the later humanist tradition, corresponds to Kermode's more archaeological probing of similarly "secular," that is, universal narrative traits and motifs in Mark which are intertextually linked with ancient traditions of fabulation.

In any case, those members of Harvard's Divinity faculty who happened to drop in on Frank Kermode's first lecture were startled not only to hear the word "hermeneutics" and references to Hermes but also almost immediately to find central importance assigned to Jesus' enigmatic saying in the Gospel of Mark about parables and the hiding of their mystery. A little later, after hearing unexpected references to *kerygma,* the Dead Sea Scrolls and the Gnostic library of Nag Hammadi, they really sat up in their chairs when the lecturer proceeded, "I come now to the performance I have undertaken, which is to speak mainly of the Gospel narratives, especially Mark."

In his second lecture, Kermode went on to discuss Jesus' parables and his sayings about their purpose, with special attention to Mark's *hina* and Matthew's *hoti.* In Mark, Jesus speaks in parables *so that* those outside may see and not perceive; in Matthew, *because* they see without perceiving. And in his third lecture we found to our delight how extensively our critic had done his homework on recent Gospel study as we heard him invoking not only Austin Farrer, Vincent Taylor, D.E. Nineham and other works on Mark but also Morton Smith and Hans Frei.

Here and in the concluding chapters there is a great deal of close attention to many texts in the Gospels and to many aspects of early Christian interpretation and canonization. The degree of expertise and the extent of background commanded by the author as evident in his discussions and notes are truly astonishing. The treatment of detail in the Gospel pericopes and the probing of familiar issues in criticism and exegesis would soon betray such a supposed newcomer to the field if he were not well grounded by a wide range of acquaintance with the relevant authorities.

That one should be surprised at this kind of resourcefulness in our discipline by a literary critic is perhaps invidious. But two considerations go far to justify it. The special domain of sacred scripture, especially the New Testament, has long remained outside the purview of our humanistic study of letters. These texts, moreover, require and have evoked so special and so labyrinthine an investigation that, as with some oriental literatures, they could well be bracketed even in the agenda of comparative literature.

In his preface and at other points (for example, in the first lecture, pages 15–16) Kermode speaks of his own motivations in this undertaking. In the past few years he had found himself increasingly concerned with problems of interpretation—especially with respect to narrative—and it was this preoccupation which "stimulated my interest in biblical exegesis and hermeneutics." Traditionally it has been biblical exegesis which has elaborated most systematically the rules and procedures of interpretation or hermeneutics.

> Until quite recently secular scholars in America and England paid very little attention to the subject, and all the major developments were of German origin. Nor has secular literary criticism shown much interest in biblical criticism, except when it has seemed essential to research of the more antiquarian kinds.

The author thinks this is unfortunate. "The scholarly quality and discipline of the best biblical study is high enough to be, in many ways, exemplary to us." Moreover, in the case of biblical interpretation it is possible to observe with special clarity the operation of those cultural or institutional constraints which are always operative in a tradition, literary or devout. Yet biblical criticism has had its own special motivating commitment leading to "a visible difference of interest and manner from almost all secular criticism" (p. viii).

> Of late, however, biblical critics have been looking over the fence and noting the methods and achievements of the secular arm; sacred and profane texts are more than ever before discussed in the same book or article. For a secular critic to work on the reserved sacred texts, as I

have chosen to do, is rarer. It is easy to understand why this should be so: there is a lack of interest (which I deplore but recognize), and there is a lack of the necessary skills. The volume of scholarship is dismaying, and any outsider is bound to make mistakes.

But, the author here concludes, "I think the gospels need to be talked about by critics of a quite unecclesiastical formation" (p. ix).

In his first lecture Kermode elaborates a little upon this theme.

It is common enough for the professionals, the exegetes *de metier,* to maintain that a correct understanding of the New Testament may be had only by the faithful; the outsiders will see without perceiving, hear without understanding. I suppose the positions can be reconciled but that is not my business. Ecclesiastical institutions are, like others, understandably anxious to protect themselves against impious intruders. Such persons are in any case unlikely to know enough in a merely technical sense, spiritual illumination apart. Yet they are, though secular, the heirs of the exegetical and hermeneutic traditions. Scrupulosity of method, subtlety of understanding and explication, the general philosophy of interpretation as it is developed in the New Testament tradition, may seem to them part of their just birthright. They should be allowed their secular say on the cardinal texts. (pp. 15–16)

There is one other observation of our author about his approach which should be mentioned. "Not in my brief" is his comment on a kind of interpretation, theological, valuational or normative, which would carry him outside his secular, literary inquiry. Whether such a "secular, literary inquiry" can be easily set off from wider valuational considerations is a matter which may well interest us further.

THE ROUND HILL CONFERENCE

In 1969 at "Round Hill," a Jesuit center on Buzzards Bay in Massachusetts, a conference on theology and literature was held under the auspices of Boston College. There Frank Kermode, John Coulson, Daniel Jenkins and other British scholars joined with American critics including Cleanth Brooks, William Wimsatt and Hillis Miller and theologians Walter Ong, Robert Funk, Sallie McFague, Arthur McGill, David Tracy, Tom Driver and J.A. Appleyard, the convener. One moment of the discussions very pertinent to Kermode's book remains vivid. Robert Funk, James M. Robinson and others of us tried in vain to argue our British visitors out of their view that Jesus' parables as he spoke them had an allegorical character. If Jesus speaks of a "father" or a "King" it must refer to God, and if of a "shepherd" or "vineyard" he must be referring to Old Testament prototypes. We could agree that there might be marginal echoes in some cases but urged that the generic force and narrative integrity of Jesus' "fictions" would be betrayed by such displacement of their import. Jesus' parables were "secular," not theocratically allegorical, even though ultimately they might bear on the Kingdom of God.

In the course of our discussion it became evident, in any case, that in the literary tradition of our guests the category of allegory had a wide usage, indicating merely some further or alternative meaning. We had thought of allegory in terms of Spenser's *The Fairie Queene* or of what Mark does with Jesus' parable of the Sower. But the point that Kermode and his colleagues were missing was that Jesus' parables, more than having some double sense, were *revelatory tropes,* inaugural visions. They were metaphors, not allegories. Even this may not go far enough. Charles Hedrick has recently urged that a metaphor points to some known correlative or point of comparison, while Jesus, like a poet, was evoking (whether as the Kingdom of God or otherwise) some uncharted reality.

Of course in his later lectures Kermode was chiefly concerned with Mark's reading of Jesus' sayings as reported in Mark 4. But we may well find here some carryover of the earlier allegorizing view of the parables. Indeed, this is one occasion in which our author, at least in his notes, raises the historical question about Jesus' teaching and, with assists from such British scholars as David Daube and John Drury (who here follows C.F.D. Moule), argues against the current critical consensus with regard to Jesus' parables: that is, that he spoke to be understood and to carry conviction. Mark for his own purposes takes advantage of the fact that especially in its Semitic background the category "parable" is wide enough to include both anecdote and riddle.

PARABLE, METAPHOR, ALLEGORY

It is worth pausing a moment over this question as to the actual functioning of Jesus' parables as he spoke them. One finds no grounds here for deliberate mystification. As witness to his generation the historical parabler was no mere pundit who could spend his time playing with tropes and fabrications and teasing his hearers with riddles. With God's cause at issue and his own life on the line he conveyed his vision in part by images and illustrations for those who had ears to hear and dispositions to respond. While his parables as one aspect of their rhetorical appeal had features of shock and disorientation, yet their import was self-revealing (as in poetry) and not something to be laboriously decoded.

Although our author's concern is with Mark as a text and not with the historical parabler, he appears to assign to the original parables the same riddle character which he finds attributed to them in Mark. This may be a hangover from the allegorizing tradition abetted by some of his scholarly mentors. More likely it is of a piece with his general view of narrative as always open and patient to many interpretations. But while Jesus' parables no doubt had a flexible resonance varying with the hearer and situation, they were in the utterance too urgent and demanding to be either opaque or open gratuitously to any reading. And while they may have evoked analogies or echoes from traditional sayings they were too creative and plastic to have their sense exhausted at the level of allegory.

Though the original parables of Jesus did receive many interpretations in the tradition, as well exemplified in what Mark does with them, they do not support the idea that all narrative is open-ended. No doubt fabulation of any kind whether in stories or in poetry does not have the one-dimensional reference we look for in much prose. *But the imagination can have its own kind of specific predication.*

NARRATIVE AND INTENTIONALITY

It seems to me that this critic's partiality for an allegorizing sense with respect to Jesus' narratives has wider implications for his total inquiry and method. We may recall that his initial axiom about narrative is that it is always open to and invites interpretation; indeed, any story solicits various readings. The corollary of this is that any particular meaning of a story, whether myth, parable or novel, can only be one option among others. All narrative is open to construction or decoding and by the same token is enigmatic and undecidable. Any claim to a particular interpretation of a narrative will therefore be suspect as motivated by the interests of the reader or group or institution in question.

This rationale of narrative is evidently encouraged if not mandated by critical insistence on the relative autonomy of the narrative text. The reader is constrained by the intratextual world and logic of the fiction in question. This focus disparages any considerations bearing on the meaning of the fable from outside the text. Such intrusions on its autonomy might include reference to the intention of the narrator or historical and social considerations which might appear relevant to the world of the recital. The issues of this vexed question of intra- and extra-textuality are still unsettled, and Jacques Derrida himself has declared emphatically that he is still very much concerned with the problem of "referentiality." But on the whole Kermode deals with the weave and peripeties of Mark's narrative in the light of their intratextual constraints and narrative logic. It is at these points that he makes his contributions to our appreciation of this Gospel, but the premises of his method unduly restrict their scope.

With his axiom about narrative as open, undecidable, enigmatic, one can appreciate his choice of the Gospel of Mark for his venture into Scripture. With its view of Jesus' parables as riddles to the outsiders and of his teaching generally as falling on deaf ears even of the insiders, this Gospel falls "pat to his purpose." His interest is in the interpretation of narrative, and Mark offers him a showpiece for the dilemmas of interpretation, for the polarity of insider and outsider, and for the "genesis of secrecy" as prerogative of the insiders.

In his book the author backgrounds his analysis of Mark's ambiguity or *aporia* with two instances drawn from modern fiction exhibiting the frustration of the interpreter. As a frontispiece in his first chapter, entitled "Carnal and Spiritual Senses," he rehearses a brilliant and tantalizing novel of Henry Green, a choice which surely weights the scales. Here we see how clues and signals in a narrative, planted by the author or read in by the reader, can point to any number of implications in the work. Narrative opens up mazes of inviting interpretations. Hares are set running in the imagination of the reader in all directions. Thus it is implied that the real interest of narration lies not in the carnal "obvious and sequential sense" but in the spiritual luxuriance of intuitive meanings and "divinations" which are opened up. Kermode has such a good time with this plethora of optional readings that one is reminded of Roland Barthes's sheer *plaisir du texte*. The link of this exercise with the Gospel of Mark is suggested: efforts to identify its "obvious and sequential sense" will only lead to bafflement. But the story Mark tells has its occult clues and signals, its "broken surfaces" and structural antinomies which invite "divination," suggesting limitless excursions into a vast echo chamber of implications.

Another recurrent backdrop invoked by our author is Kafka's well-known parable, as it is called, of the petitionary at the Gate of the Law. His frustration as he dies after a lifetime of attendance at the gate now closed to him is hardly compensated for by his glimpse of the radiancy within. Here again, that the law or the sacred narrative or the world itself cannot be deciphered appears to have its warrant in Mark's austere and enigmatic Gospel.

Any demurrer to Kermode's sobering assessment will have to deal both with his basic view of narrative and with his analysis of Mark. With respect to narrative one can agree that it invites interpretation and that it does not make such specific monosemeic statement as much discursive exposition seeks. But narratives differ. Naturally a novel like that of Henry Green, though it is not an exercise in mystification, exploits the ambivalencies and options common to all sign systems. Gratuity and fortuity have every encouragement in its interpretation. But our species has had to use language and signs for the grim purposes of orientation, consensus and survival and so has had to learn controls over their vagaries. This applies also to our narrative traditions. Like maxims and aphorisms, stories and epics have *meant one thing rather than another,* even though they were not discursive statements. Indeed, just because they were not discursive they could make statements and provide information that were all the more significant. Granted that, as narrative, there is still room in such texts for interpretation, yet all such glossing, explanation and application will be *controlled* (as well as nourished) by the original thrust of the text, at the same time that unwarranted intrusions are excluded. This seemingly intolerant view of the meaning of the text should not be assigned to the ideological and even "political" line of defense of some institution since it goes back to the original "gestation of meaning" behind the text in question.

Kermode's view of narrative prizes in it the multiple sense, the occult meaning, decoding, allegory, paradox, the undecidable, even the mind-boggling parable or koan of Kafka or Borges.

On the other hand, that narrative and rhetorics generally can make a *particular* statement and provide a nonambiguous witness is now further confirmed by new studies in rhetoric.[1] The roots of speech, of the production of meaning and of world-making lie with *intentionality*. This underlies and governs all rhetorics. Language usages and communication are *directed*, not arbitrary or optional, directed toward human viability. This takes rhetoric, after a long detour, back to the original views of Aristotle. We should look in a fabulation or history for the discriminate intentionality of the writing which will no doubt overlap with the intentions of the writer and of the initial or implied reader.

Whether any text or narrative, fiction or history, is an open fabulation whose course is subject in a random way to anterior motifs and figurations from the language inheritance, *or* a communication oriented to speaker (author) and hearer (reader) in a shared context of experience, depends upon our view of language itself. If language is primordially intentional—with a view to orientation and the production of meaning—then any fortuitous chain of associations is like a mere spinning of the wheels of available signs. Derrida provides a full-dress illustration of this in his extended study of the work of Jean Genet in *Glas*. Here both the narrative and dramatic scenarios reflect the autonomous operations of vestigial, visceral and fetishist syndromes which have escaped control and establish their own "reality," usurping upon both the self and its "world."

If, however, language properly understood is intentional and directed, it surmounts all such nether residues in the psyche and the arbitrariness of signs associated with them. Deconstruction will still have its work to do since these and other disorders still intrude on and inhabit our perceptions and even our better grounded texts.

---

1. See Chaim Perelman, *The New Rhetoric and the Humanities,* Synthese Library 140 (Dordrecht, Boston, London, 1979); John R. Searle, *Intentionality: An Essay in the Philosophy of Mind* (New York: Cambridge University Press, 1983). See also, as regards New Testament topics, the following by Wilhelm Wuellner: "The Rhetorical Structure of Luke 12 in Its Wider Context," *Neotestamentica* 22 (1989): 283–310; "Is There an Encoded Reader Fallacy?" in *Readers' Perspectives on the New Testament,* ed. Edgar V. McKnight, *Semeia* 48 (Atlanta: Scholars Press, 1989); *Hermeneutics and Rhetorics: From "Truth and Method" to "Truth and Power,"* Scriptura S 3 (Stellenbosch, South Africa: Centre for Hermeneutical Studies, 1989); "Where is Rhetorical Criticism Taking Us?" *Catholic Biblical Quarterly* 49:448–63.

READING MARK'S STORY

I turn now to my demurrer to Kermode's analysis of Mark, an analysis which indeed agrees with his understanding of narrative. Is this Gospel as enigmatic as he sees it? He himself recognizes that in its first verse it identifies itself as a heralding of Good News. But this must be some kind of paradox! I myself think that like many others this reader misconstrues the "hard saying" of Mark 4:11-12.

Without asking him to step outside "the world of the text" can he not agree that this dealing with the reprobate, this blinding of their perceptions, fits well at this point, and that Jesus' speaking in parables, here as riddles, has special and limited reference to the occasion? We have just read that the authorities were planning to destroy him (3:3) and had charged him with being in league with Satan. This controversy already anticipates his later condemnation and crucifixion. Thus Mark sees Jesus retrospectively in the same fated role as that of Isaiah, pleading in vain for the repentance of his people as it confronts, now in an even greater crisis, national disaster and the destruction of the temple. As Isaiah saw the outcome retrospectively in terms of the prophetic appeal and its rejection and consequent doom in the light of predestination, so Mark sees Jesus' appeal to his generation, its rejection, and national disaster from the point of view of the embattled new community, all again in terms of God's ordination. In this typology based on Isaiah which Mark follows, Jesus' parables take on the penal function of Isaiah's prophecies. Outside this context in Mark, however, the parables of Jesus, like his teaching generally, had no such riddling and damning character.

As I have observed, his mission was too urgent for puzzles or mystification. His tropes and parables were intended for clarification and served the purposes of effective debate. When this teacher, warning against hypocrisy, said, "Let your 'yes' be 'yes' and your 'no' 'no'," we can recognize the norm of his parables.

The upshot of these observations is that one should not appeal to Jesus' parables to argue that Mark's Gospel is enigmatic. Even as presented in Mark—apart from the ad hoc hyperbolic typological use in 4:11-12—the parables, like Jesus' saving actions and whole demeanor, dramatize his mission. "He that hath ears to hear, let him hear." The sayings are not hard to understand. The scribes "perceived that the saying [the parable] was spoken against them."

Whether in the case of the authorities or the disciples themselves as the evangelist saw it, incomprehension was due to hardness of heart and not to obscurity in the parables.

Kermode understandably finds other aspects of Mark's narrative which support his view that like all narrative it is open to differing interpretations and therefore undecipherable and "unfollowable." On the surface of the recital he deals delightfully with the recognized anomaly of the episode of the youth who flees unclad in the Garden of Gethsemane. He also exposes those procedures, all too familiar, by which the narrator confers historical verisimilitude upon an account and the manipulation of Old Testament texts to lend credence to his story. All in all the heterogeneous character of Mark's material, with the overlapping of its several generic legacies, argues for an indeterminacy in the writing which in fact appears to be sanctioned by the narrator himself with his view of Jesus deliberately speaking in riddles. This baffling import of the narration is only too clearly confirmed by the inconclusive way it ends at 16:8 in comparison with our other Gospels: no evident closure, no Resurrection appearance, the disciples in disarray, no seal on what was announced as a publishing of salvation at the beginning.

One can understand Kermode's recourse in dealing with such a narrative. Meaning is to be sought not in any sequential logic but by way of "intermittent radiancies" flashing out from deeper strata and structural legacies as he illustrates by reference to the "intercalations" which are so marked a feature of Mark's composition. Here, on the analogy of Kafka's parable, the "outsider" can exercise his own divination in penetrating that secret whose import Mark and his Elect have claimed as their prerogative.

But this Gospel is not so baffling. Its public readability for its time does indeed appeal to several generic modes, including what we would call "biographical" anecdote and portrayal in the biblical tradition and the Hellenistic hero model. But these are taken up and transformed in an equally familiar eschatological visionary model. This world-drama reaches back to Elijah, Moses and the Patriarchs and forward beyond the time of the author to that closure associated with the manifestation of the Son of Man and cosmic regeneration. Mark is a reading of world destiny. "Mark writes a particular kind of history, which may be called a narration of the course of the eschatological events, which are yet to be completed. (Thus the open-endedness of the ending.)"[2] It is because Mark writes during the final "tribulation" when his community was persecuted, reviewing the operations of Satan in the course of Jesus' ministry, that his dialectic of "insider" and "outsider" is so sharp, and the rejection of Jesus' teaching is seen as so fateful. Though Mark sees his whole theocratic-eschatological history in mythical terms, yet the realism and even secularity with which he evokes aspects of Jesus' mission and teaching styles (related to current popular "bios" modes with their itineraries, encounters, dialogues, *chriai* and marvels) reflect the fact that his eschatological drama is rooted in mundane circumstance and empirical transactions.

In this perspective the peripeties of Mark's history, despite its heterogeneous sources, gaps and broken surface, are not "unfollowable." Incomprehension of and antagonism to Jesus' proclamation and radical antinomies with respect to his ultimate horizon of the new era—these are, indeed, features of the evangelist's total scenario. Seemingly irreconcilable contradictions and anomalies block any consecutive logic in the plot: the stultification of the many, the inversion of Jesus' true family, the clairvoyance of the demons, the shifts of the Revealer from public disclosure to withdrawal and secrecy, the dereliction of the chosen. Yet Mark sees his whole story not as a cryptogram but as open and crowning disclosure.

While it is written from the point of view of the "elect" or insiders of his community, yet the evangelist recognizes that their response was anticipated by a remnant in the days of Jesus' ministry. Indeed, Mark's arraignment of the "outsiders" as doomed may, as in the case of Isaiah and many later preachers of predestination, be seen as a rhetorical call to repentance, still open in these last days during which he writes!

Why is Frank Kermode's reading so far apart from the one I have proposed? I would insist that, at least up to this point, it is not a question of confessional premise on my part. By literary-critical criteria alone I believe that Kermode's quiver of strategies does not equip him for this kind of text. The most damaging lapse arises at the crux of generic appraisal. This is surprising in view of this author's

2. Adela Yarbro Collins, "Narrative, History and Gospel," *Semeia* 43 (1988): 148.

initiation into matters of genre. This is evident in his long note on the topic (chap. 6, n. 20, pp. 162–63). Again, more recently, he discusses genre with reference to such writings as Mark in *Semeia* 43, "Anteriority, Authority and Secrecy," pp. 155–67.

Kermode, indeed, recognizes the variety if not of identifiable genres in Mark at least of culturally shaped rhetorical modes which help establish the readability of the narrative. Mark did not belong to an established genre but was, as has been said, a "host-genre." But among these generic patterns Kermode does not assign to the eschatological one its definitive function, and this accounts for much of the dissonance he finds in the narration. From its first verse—the Greek term *euangelion* evokes not only biblical but pagan (Vergil, Horace, Statius) auguries of the new age—this Gospel builds on its myth of conflict and salvation, and adapts his other "genres" to it.

In Mark's weave the apocalyptic pattern is not just our orientation to the total architectonics of the Gospel. As functioning genre it *enables* the reader to identify himself affectively with the teleological vicissitudes of the plot: expectations, hopes, fears, devotion and betrayal, praise and shame. This focusing and structuring of Mark comes within the purview of literary criticism, attentive to generic and intratextual appraisal, and need not wait on historicizing or theological criteria. This is one occasion to say, however, that the literary criticism of the Bible will not make its full contribution to the study of the canon until it throws its light on those aspects of rhetoric which it now sees as "not in its brief." To put the matter in shorthand, this would mean dealing not only with the aesthetic categories of *beauty* and *form* but with the theological category of *glory!*

TEXT AND HISTORY

If narrative is ultimately "intentional" and "suasive," this undercuts any strict view of the autonomy of the text. The implicit thrust of discourse, back to its origins in naming, signifying and imaging, represents a selective engagement with the givens of experience and the pursuit of meaning amid the maze of alternatives. Storying prolongs this basically pragmatic function. "Narrative worlds" are penetrated by empirical actuality not only in this initial grounding but also in their seemingly fictional inventions. When post-modern writers aspire to some form of "pure" fabulation or free exploitation of the language medium, the resulting exercise draws its force not intrinsically but solely by reverberation of the very norm it seeks to elude.

With regard to this issue as to the extratextual referentiality of narrative Kermode is inclined with Jean Starobinski (pp. 135–36) to look in Mark for "what is written" in distinction from "what is written about." This means attending to the text without being distracted by questions as to its context and reference, historical or ideological. Since the Gospel falls so far short of presenting a "well-shaped narrative" we should, on this view, take our cue rather from its recurrent features of antinomy and paradox and seek to identify some deeper "algebra" charged with a recondite meaning.

In the case of Mark we can certainly be instructed by thus honoring the autonomy of the text. But this autonomy cannot be absolute. That "no narrative can be transparent on historical fact" does not mean that all links with our human experience, all resonances, are excluded. The very act of reading involves a correlation of text and life and therefore some prior referentiality of the text. The issues here become specially acute with the recent critical school which deepens the gulf in question by urging the sedimentation of all our inherited frames of perception and interpretation, and beyond that by its radical epistemological skepticism.

Kermode in his fifth chapter ("What Precisely Are the Facts?") writes that he "cannot go so far." What I have called his minimalist hermeneutic holds that our passion to explain calls at the very least for ventures in divination. He thinks that we are driven by a compulsion to interpret which, even when confronted as here with seeming contradictions and mystery, prompts us to this at least. As clues in the contradictions of Mark's text he lights therefore upon those intercalations of episodes, those "analepses," in which antinomies and conjunctions can be recognized. But this feature, as he sees it, is paradigmatic for the Gospel as a whole! For is not this writing itself intercalated between *arche* and *telos,* between origin and consummation? The secret of the Gospel may thus be exposed as ultimate (and layered) antinomy, which is nevertheless a provocation to wonder, to further query and to fabulation.

Why our author has unnecessarily gone so far afield can be illustrated by the way he deals with Mark's so-called Little Apocalypse, chapter 13. This prediction made privately by Jesus of the signs and birthpangs and accomplishment of the consummation can be seen as an intercalation between the ministry of Jesus and the Passion narrative which follows. Actually it is here and in Jesus' crowning pronouncement before the authorities at his trial of the coming of the Son of Man in glory that this Gospel has its real closure. Thus one can recognize the eschatological genre as the warp upon which the entire narrative of Mark is woven. But Kermode like many others mistakes this horizon of the discourse, thus depriving the Gospel of its fulfillment, and can only see that baffling last scene in Mark 16 which he therefore counts as one of its enigmas.

But what our critic finds as unduly enigmatic in Mark's story can be traced to other misreadings apart from this major issue of genre. I have already pointed to his misunderstanding of the way in which the evangelist presents Jesus' teaching in parables. Even more fundamental is our author's skepticism with regard to Mark's rootedness in what we call history. Little or no continuity between past and present is admitted, nor is the tenacity of social memory. He holds that the "generic set" or frame of perception and reporting of the inaugural events of the Gospel are so buried as to be far beyond our recovery. Thus we have a truncation of our links over the generations with the past as well as radical skepticism with regard to Mark's reporting.

Now note that this historiographical skepticism is correlated with and appears to be confirmed by current views of the "autonomy of the text" of which I have spoken. Even if this linguistic-critical thesis is qualified by Kermode it nevertheless deepens the gap between Mark's record and the historical transaction which occasioned it. As a result the text, the narration, is read apart from the *meaning* of those transactions, that meaning which it was the evangelist's main purpose to establish.

Mark's narrative has, indeed, its semantic background in familiar genres, *topoi,* figurations, all of which furthered its readability at the time. But its story is not tied to these heterogeneous motifs. Nor in its autonomy (as is expected of texts) does it pursue its own random and fortuitous chain of associations. This portrayal of the end-time travail and consummation is controlled by the actual historical drama reported over a scale which reaches from immediate observation to appropriate imaginative witness. There is no gulf between "what is written," and "what is written about." Whatever secret lies behind the rehearsal, it is an open secret. There are, indeed, antinomies deeply inscribed in it, but they are the ultimate antagonism of light and darkness, God and Satan, which are overcome in the Gospel and the community.

Attention may be drawn here to a strange lacuna in those studies directed to text and fabulation. In their exposure of the illogics and incoherence so recurrent a feature of much discourse and narrative, the question does not seem to be raised as to differences in intention and urgency of speech. It should be recognized that in some writings the role of vagary, inattention, the oneiric and latent intrusions is minimized or excluded. Some communication is so focused and charged with meaning that diversity in its sources is subsumed and plurisignification in its horizon is controlled. It is distinctive of the oracles and logos of Israel among human cultures that they represent a unique *grip on reality* and one which carries over into the writings of our Christian canon.

What is at stake in all these literary-rhetorical inquiries into Mark's narrative is the issue as to its purport and cogency as a communication. The question of cogency involves both that of the coherence of the recital and its responsiveness to our human actuality and questing, first of all for those readers for whom it was written. But this responsiveness required a realistic engagement with their empirical circumstance and "history." Mark's task therefore was to provide a reading of the shocking historical events of the Gospel story while recasting them in a meaningful frame.

It follows that Mark's preternatural narrative is saturated with and controlled by "history." His "text," indeed, can be read in terms of its own inherent continuity as story. But the question of its referentiality, of what is "inside" or "outside" the text, still calls for clarification. The answer lies in what we have learned about language and the "generation of meaning." Meaning, indeed, requires signs, requires language. But meaning in language emerges and is established in response to actuality and its prompting. Meaningful discourse, texts, narrative therefore represent a merging of empirical actuality— including its prelinguistic and protolinguistic aspects—with language. In a narrative like that of the Gospel of Mark the *realia* in question are not first a matter of mimesis or referentiality but are mediated in the text itself.[3]

If we are asking, therefore, about the historical dimension and reliability of Mark's Gospel we have to do both with that substratum of realistic data reported and the visionary frame within which they find a place.

As regards those data, their importance is in keeping with that basic feature of Israel's mentality which from the beginning was rooted in a somatic empirical anthropology. Mark has no docetic or noumenal premise. In keeping with this realism Mark's account is initially concerned with actual happenings, with a disturbance in the quotidian life of a province on the fringe of the *Oecumene*. In this respect his world-epos is rooted in ultimate givens of time and place in the flux of experience and amid the brutal commonplaces of power and weakness, order and disorder, good and evil. This original engagement with the actualities of the world and its course continues throughout the entire narrative so that even its mythic overlays are penetrated by it.

If we speak thus of an original stratum of empirical reporting in the Gospel, if not of eyewitness record, we are rightly cautioned that all so-called facts are always already interpreted. While therefore we do not have a chronicle of facts even at this initial level, yet Mark's tradition evokes an underpinning in the Gospel of transactions in time and place which anchor his whole structure. In this respect one may say that his narrative is "transparent" upon real happenings in the world of that time.

---

3. In his book *Radical Hermeneutics: Repetition, Deconstruction, and the Hermeneutic Problem* (Bloomington: Indiana University Press, 1987) John Caputo discusses "the generation of meaning" in a way which illuminates the foregoing. He traces the views on this topic from Kierkegaard through Husserl and Heidegger to Derrida. World-making, the generation of self, world and meaning, arises out of the human need and impulsion to arrest and give pattern to the basic flux of experience. Throughout, the establishment of sense and meaning, the constitution of viable unities, proceeds by way of merging intention and expectancy with already achieved horizons. Thus those language patterns and narratives which have been established are continually revised by the original thrust. The whole process is indeed continually undermined by the instabilities of the self, and Derrida here highlights most searchingly the ambiguities and mistaken byways of the quest. But what I would stress here is the ultimate pragmatic motivation of the interpretive project, and the conjointness throughout of the "world of the text" with living experience.

Turning now to what I have called the visionary frame in which Mark sets his initial empirical givens, we can ask about its historical bearings. What we have in view here is what in our categories we would call the mythic charting of his world-plot, all those features of his portrayal which constitute it finally as a preternatural narrative. One should observe first that the writing is all of a piece. As I have noted, the initial engagement with *realia,* in the writer's view, pervades the whole. All those overtones or extrapolations of the brute data which we see as mythological and groundless are aspects of Mark's total witness, related throughout to situation and actuality. The surreal aspects of the recital are required by, and answer to, the opposed *realia,* cultural and mythological, of the setting. As "gospel" Mark's narrative portrays at this depth the throes and eventual prevailing of salvation, not in "spiritual" terms but in the embattled historical arena of the epoch. In this respect, therefore, we can recognize that Mark's narrative here also is "transparent" on history.

To illustrate this pragmatic and culture-historical dimension of Mark's portrayal, I would point to the following. (One finds a parallel reading of mundane circumstance, political and ideological, in John's Apocalypse.) I have already indicated that the horizon evoked by Mark's term *euangelion* would have had pagan-imperial as well as biblical resonance for his readers. In many respects the Christology of the Gospel likewise had its links with the cultural dream of Hellenistic society, as exemplified in the words of the centurion at the foot of the Cross, "Truly this man was the Son of God!"

A striking example of the visionary frame in which Mark sets his record is that of the Transfiguration episode. This parenthesis in the account of the ministry links the mission of Jesus with the historical roles of Moses and Elijah in a way which grounds his own role in this present greater controversy of God with his people. Thus the evangelist lifts his recital and widens his horizon to include both the annals and theophanies of Israel and the travail and auguries of the empire. Indeed, he can revert to Adam, the father of all humankind: "In the beginning it was not so" (speaking of divorce). And I for one am persuaded that behind his evocation of the Son of Man, despite its later variables, lay this universal progenitor. Behind Mark's Son of David, Messiah, Lord, is the Son of God of the creation itself.

This universalism of Mark and his implied readers is illustrated again by another mythical overlay in his bifocal history, that of the operations of Satan, the Adversary, and the demons. At the very beginning after Jesus hears the voice from heaven, "Thou art my beloved Son," like Adam he "was tempted of Satan." This ultimate antinomy in the drama recurs in the exorcisms, in the rebuke of Peter, in the *peirasmos* or temptation in the Lord's prayer, and all the way through to "the abomination of desolation" preceding the final judgment. Here again Mark provides a surreal reading of the impasses and travail associated with the birth of the new age.

One further note is called for as to the bearing of such a view on current issues as to "text" in its relation to what may be "outside" it. I have cited the passage in which Frank Kermode is inclined (as is Jean Starobinski in his reading of Mark's account of Jesus' cure of the Gerasene demoniac) to read "what is written" in distinction from "what is written about." Meaning, we are again reminded, requires signs, that is, language. Apart from language, therefore, that is, outside the world of the text, there is no "other," no reference. Many like Kermode will not go so far, but for him this critique in any case disallows the "carnal, obvious and sequential reading of the narrative."

It is true that meaning is inseparable from signs and their distinctions. But how can one read signs, and their assemblage in language, without taking account of what they signify? To read "what is written" apart from "what is written about" is correspondingly misguided. To adhere to the text in a supposed faithfulness to the letter and out of fear of misprision is to condemn oneself to an empty exercise. In fact those who pursue it find their own kinds of meaning where nothing is supposedly signified.

Technically, the procedure is defended by evoking the "arbitrariness" of the sign. Signifieds, meanings, are consequently devalued. But that signs (here in the sense of "signifiers") are arbitrary is an abstract relational observation when made in this technical linguistic context. This does not take account of the life-situation of naming, positing, distinguishing in which an urgent, pragmatic intentionality operates. In *this* context "signifieds" are important and stable in the functioning of language. Here we can recognize the production and

spiritual and ethical impulses like that of the Romantic movement. After the sobering ordeal of the Great War and the related disorders of both social authority and the higher culture, the terms were set for an overdue clarification of the ancient pieties and their relation to the cultural *anomie* and its arts and literature.

One example of this new confrontation was the work of T.S. Eliot with both his archaeology of the past in *The Waste Land* and his witness to a purgative Christian faith in *Four Quartets*. Another is the sharp feuding in France in the early twenties between Catholic novelists and pamphleteers like Mauriac and Bernanos with the secular and anticlerical writers of the time.

It was not therefore surprising that in this country, when the genteel era of the post-Victorians was over, and with the advent of such writers as Hart Crane and Conrad Aiken, Hemingway and Dos Passos and Faulkner, American interest in the vicissitudes of the religious tradition should have been alerted. So we saw the emergence of what was called "theology and literature" or "religion and the arts." This could be a dogmatic testing of particular writers, but since the formulation of the faith was itself in question and the values of secularized culture were to be respected, it meant rather a searching scrutiny of the creative writers in view, both their witness to embattled values and their vagaries. This inquest could extend itself back to precursors in the New World scene as notably to those who had registered the various facets of American Puritanism. All this represented on the part of the theologically oriented critics a sifting of the deeper fealties of our society. Recognizing that many of the uncanonical artists of the time were more deeply initiated into its costs than apologists for the religious institutions—were in some cases revelatory victims of the situation—one could not but concede that they were often ahead of the churchmen in illuminating the realities of the age.

This opening up of the creative and moral options on the scene with its testimonies to a secular exploration, or even to what Cocteau called a *mystère laic,* prompted the faithful to a more relevant understanding of their tradition in its relation to the cultural disarray. Thus a meaningful dialogue could be furthered with the dissident quests among the most sensitive interpreters or barometers of the occasion. In fact, many of these alienated artists evidence in various ways their roots in the religious past, and this nostalgia betrayed itself in their fabulation.

This attention to the vicissitudes of our cultural traditions then spread to our academic departments and forums. Scholars could not deny the more-than-aesthetic import of many of the modern classics with which they had to deal in their classrooms. In the college and the university, however, the distinctive theological legacy was subsumed under the general category of religion. In a neutral and humanist context a particular theological movement like that of Puritanism or the doctrines of Roman Catholicism could be identified, but under the constraints of the social sciences their import could be obscured or relativized as religious ideology.

This antidogmatic and anticonfessional approach was also encouraged by new interest in Eastern religions and a general disparagement of divisiveness, whether as regards such faiths or our differing cults at home. This ecumenical sensitivity prompted in part by relativism and indifferentism together with the academic canons mentioned meant, however, that the preponderant role in our culture of the biblical tradition was slighted. Its trajectories in the modern period and its particular premises in the mosaic of religion and creative ferment fell outside of the valuable canvass of religious phenomenology of our society. Another way to put this is to say that the legacy of the prophets of Israel and its transmission through synagogue and church, with their critique of culture, were homogenized with other conflicting pieties, mythologies, cults and utopias in the folkways.

Thus the initial venture of "theology and literature" became the less challenging program of "religion and the arts." The original concern with criteria continued in even secular instances. In the 1940s Alfred Barr of the Museum of Modern Art became the president of the Society for the Arts, Religion and Contemporary Culture. As one brought up in a devout home, he was concerned that the arts of the religious bodies should be purified in keeping with their calling, having in view the sentimentality, chromos and *bondieuserie* with which they were so widely infected. Other associates of the society like W.H. Auden, Denis de Rougemont and Paul Tillich similarly pressed the critical function of this tradition in confronting either the Philistinism or the more superficial cults and religiosities of our society.

The austere claims of this tradition were, however, even more obscured in the sixties, the Age of Aquarius, when both the youth culture and elements of the higher culture were captivated by a wave of liberations, visceral and orgiastic, psychic and oneiric, social and ideological. For its symbolic motifs this euphoria appealed to exotic models, often displaced and misunderstood: from Amerindian and Zen Buddhist to the wisdom of Hindu adepts and Mexican sorcery. More deeply, it reflected a passion for the limitless, the arcane and the Absolute. In its more perfervid aspect, as in its association with Maoism, it delegitimized all authority including that of the university. In a discussion of post-modernism I cited as an epilogue the graffito scrawled on the walls of the Faculté des Lettres at the University of Nanterre (over which Paul Ricoeur had at one time presided): *Méfiez-vous de l'abyssal autant que du céleste.*

In the sequel of the carnival of the sixties it is true that many of the vaporous impulses subsided. Nevertheless, awareness of the whole order of social myths and dreams, of mystiques and gnosticisms, in short, the imaginative repertoire of the culture, absorbed the attention of those concerned with religion and the arts, at the expense of a more critical appraisal. Such names as those of Alan Watts and Joseph Campbell indicate the focus of attention, the one representing the emancipated quests of a rootless generation, and the other the appeal of the dynamic and erotic categories of Carl Jung and the Eranos circle. This transcultural repertoire has had a continuing and plausible correspondence with one-world perspectives. But the proclaimed pluralism of the alienated reflects a contemporary spirituality which has failed to wrestle with its antecedents and with its stubborn empirical context.

The foregoing retrospect could have included the ideology of Marxism among the various dissident mythologies of the period. Its utopianism, however, tended to merge with other liberations in our arts and letters. The case of Kenneth Patchen is here illustrative. At first a perfervid Communist, he later became a lifelong iconoclast appealing to eclectic motifs in his texts and accompanying brushwork.

One can also ask about where the mainline religious bodies and their people fit into this review. If we speak of theology and culture one must recognize that the faithful in church and synagogue, if only by their social class, had been sheltered from many of the stresses of the time. No doubt their pieties made room for various worldly intrusions, notably the idols of tribe and marketplace. If all this was true of the mainline churches it was even more so of the entrenched Bible

Belt. Indeed, its literalist fundamentalism could be recognized as the secularization of an earlier robust piety, overlaid as it was with a rationalist armature taken over from the unbelievers.

While our religious groups had their social prophets it was at the point of psychic disorder that their securities were most deeply disturbed by the new forces. The gap between inherited constraints and the new disabused climate of secular exploration was particularly felt in the personal life, in tensions associated with vocation and lifestyle, and especially with family, marriage and sexuality. But this deep-seated dilemma led many of the more perceptive in the churches to inquire further into their moral traditions.

The religious institutions should, however, be credited with their indispensable role in transmitting the major legacy of the West and its orienting vision to the new generations, whatever the deviants of that heritage.

Those concerned with religion and the arts should not, therefore, confine themselves to a descriptive, sociological or comparative scrutiny of the creativities of the age or to however appreciative a reconnoitering of its aesthetic expressions. The task is diachronic as well as synchronic. It involves the visions of the past as well as those of today. It calls for diverse initiations and competences, for sensitivities on a scale which is dissatisfied with academic categories, and therefore for criteria searching enough for such an extended purview.

In attending to the literature, rhetorics and dynamic imagery of our time there should be no segregation of the aesthetic category or of secular activity. The appraisal called for is that of all the various fabulations and unresolved quests of the time, and this includes similarly disordered versions and dramatizations of our religious tradition. For this overall analysis criteria are indispensable. Indeed, where longstanding perspectives differ, a criterion of criteria is called for. The scrutiny identified as "theology and literature" proposes such a standpoint, not as a dogmatic or imperialist approach but as a persuasive way of orienting ourselves all along the line and especially today in the fertile luxuriance of human aspirations and the consequent theater of compelling myths. Whether the myths, obsessions and oneirics of the culture are salutary and rooted in *realia* calls for discrimination. But since any such sifting meets today with highly sophisticated inquests into modern society, the theologian cannot intrude naively but must fully engage with the wisdoms of the time. It is this situation which has focused attention so widely on basic questions of language and discourse and on *hermeneia,* hermeneutics.

As in the past so today any proposed normative critique of literature like that of the theologian has a number of variables to consider. First, with respect to the texts in view: the canon both of older masterpieces and of current prestigious authors is ever-changing and presents options which require some kind of adjudication. Here as well as in religion there are partisans and chapels. Modern letters and critical schools notoriously have their various and vociferous contenders.

Again, the theological norm itself has its changing formulations, and any such lever introduced into the scenario needs to be clarified and grounded. There is no doubt some overlapping of the premises of faith and those of the secular visions represented, and the case for the former can be made more persuasive.

But there is still a third variable in the operation and one which has special importance today. "Theology and literature" has to deal not only with texts but with widely varying and tenaciously held views of method, with sophisticated theories of reading. These strategies are deeply sanctioned by the scientific premises of the academy or by revolt against them. Those who espouse them have not only ideological but ontological investments in their claims. The main point is that these methods stand between the text and the reader. The theologian meets here with issues which lead back to a fundamental understanding of language and rhetorics. This is why the topic of hermeneutics has taken on its current importance.

In view of the diversity of texts, methods and premises thus signaled it should be clear how limited and preliminary any assessment can be in terms of "religion and the arts." Forfeiting any ultimate criterion—either as a self-denying scholarly impartiality or in view of a basic commitment to relativism—this approach contents itself with a canvass and probing of the creativities manifest in modern letters. This inquisition into the cultural myths and epiphanies of the time, spiritual and aesthetic, adds a valuable dimension to a strictly sociological analysis or a conventional literary criticism. As a kind of theopoetics it calls attention to the prerational and imaginative vitalities of the period. The links of all such fabulation with societal realities may be recognized, but here, too, the premises of openness and pluralism arrest any pursuit of arbitrating criteria.

A more searching theopoetic, however, would require wider circumspections. Members of our departments of religious studies who were interested in aesthetics understandably included modern and post-modern literature in their study. As themselves products of modernity and its disarray they were attracted or even dazzled by the representative talents of this *anomie* and by the critical initiatives reflecting our age of suspicion.

This focus, however, delimited the field of observation as regards the religious dimension of literature and of culture generally. While the iconoclastic writings in question could be related to an erosion of older authorities, their links with the actual structures and moralities of everyday life were forfeited. They also represented a disjunction with the legacies of the past. The resulting forum of exploration and theopoetic thus had a rootless and floating character. This had its appeal for the disoriented in the Age of Anxiety as it pointed toward untrammeled vistas and divinations of the Absolute.

In a lecture presented by Hans Jonas attended some years ago by members of the Society for the Arts, Religion and Contemporary Culture the speaker called attention to the recurring phenomenon of Gnosticism in the history of the West. As with its sway in the first centuries of our era it appears in periods of transition between succeeding epochs of established consensus. This schema does much to illuminate the revulsion and the gratuity associated with many contemporary writings.

Of course the repertoire of such cultural phases differs, but they have certain recurring traits. Our own conjuncture recalls that of the early sixteenth century so vividly evoked by Marguerite Yourcenar in her *L'Oeuvre au noir (The Abyss)*. Among the true initiates are esoteric mystiques, theosophies and speculative erotics along with novel mythologies of the sacred, hierarchies of demonic tyrants and ineffable angels—all this reflecting a reversal of values featured in the style by antinomies and resort to the grotesque and to paradox. At a more popular level the situation is marked by an exceptional absorption in spiritualism, astrology, hallucinogenics, sorcery, antinomian rites and the cult of Satan.

It is true that in this deracinated interval many of our authors cling to tradition. It is also true that even those responsive to this climate, often identified as post-modern, can exhibit a blend of motifs and iconology. So in the Roman period there were many gnosticisms, and the faithful and the revolters alike wrestled with two worlds.

But it is this complex situation today which calls not only for description but for evaluation. Moreover, for assessment of the new voices and quests of our modern period it is not enough to hail their liberation from what may seem a stifling background. Too often even our religionists identify the welcome disenthrallments in course with their own personal history. But if only as scholars they should stand above the confusion, grounded in a perspective which can weigh both tradition and iconoclasm.

This plea should not be seen as just another appeal to the tradition and the classics. It is true again that our critics would not be so overimpressed by contemporary texts and current dialectic if their initiation into ancient epic and drama had been deeper. But the issue here is not that of heritage versus novelty. It is that of a prior human orientation and its parameters, a screen of "reader response," which tests both the ancient and the modern.

In the contemporary literary scene with its medley of poets, novelists and dramatists as well as of critical schools, the theological observer will find much to value. The talents of the time often offer a disabused scrutiny of the mores of our society which illuminates his own analysis. Their exposures of illusions and of the idols of the folkways reinforce his concerns. Even the stark tableaux of evil, reporting public inhumanities or private trauma, serve him by particularizing the enigmas with which his faith presumes to deal. I think here of lines from T.S. Eliot's *Four Quartets* ("East Coker"):

> As we grow older
> The world becomes stranger, its patterns more complicated
> Of dead and living . . .

More recent writers have further charted this bleak terrain, though few if any with the mastery of Samuel Beckett. The issue with respect to such texts, however, is not that of optimism versus pessimism, yea-saying versus negation. The charge of nihilism is too loosely invoked, and Beckett is far from being a nihilist or demolisher. What should concern us is the basic apperception and register of the artist in his reading of the human story. This perspective is properly realistic in relating the imagination to its roots in our creaturely experience. But truncation at this point is precisely the recourse of all Gnosticism and the occasion for its flights into gratuitous fabulation. These exploit the resonances of language but only as it has been severed from its available vitalities.

The newer explorations of critical method offer a similar challenge to discrimination. Here structuralist and post-structuralist investigations of discourse have alerted us to aspects of language which must be taken into account.

For my purposes the issues revolve about the functioning of words and our confidence in their reporting. The basic operations of naming, imaging and predication are in question, and this extends to storying and all rhetorics. When we confront the dismaying vicissitudes and instabilities of language we can appreciate the move in critical circles to opt for a basic indeterminism in discourse and in literary texts. One corollary of this situation is that it confirms a widespread skepticism in our modern outlook.

There is, however, a more particular literary-critical consequence of this dilemma. If meaning and reality cannot be assigned to what is named and imaged (the "signifieds") all the more importance accrues to the word itself (the "signifier") and to its autonomous operations. This priority of language over life in any case has its exemplifications in the history of cultures. Structuralists have noted the ways in which names and images, categories and oppositions, stories and myths have had a life of their own and have dictated such matters as caste and custom over long periods of stagnation. Thus criticism today is invited to assess the operation of such autonomous factors in modern life and literature.

This focus on the rhetoric or text alone apart from the mooted problem of their meaning leads some to a strictly aesthetic approach. Confining itself to the rich play of textual and intertextual figuration literary criticism resolves itself into an epicure's delectation with the world of the imagination.

Literature cannot, however, be so neatly divorced from life, nor language from actuality. Even when we recognize the vagaries of the word (remembering what Eliot said about words, that "they slip, slide" and "never stay in place") there is always some correspondence between word and world. In this disordered relation deconstruction has its opportunity. Derrida himself acknowledges that the problem of "reference" has a crucial claim. But the panorama of literature still presents us with the task of sifting out residues and intrusions of outworn mentality as well as the seductions of irreality and ideology. Short of its more presumptuous operations deconstruction has a useful work to do here. It recognizes that language has its history and its surviving constraints and that these legacies need to be identified. For an example of such archaeology I cite Derrida's *Glas* which exposes arcane motifs both in Hegel the philosopher and in Jean Genet the fabulist.

Our critical schools today, recognizing that texts are inherently linked with history, politics and morals, are not satisfied with either an aesthetic appreciation or with familiar categories such as Freudian, Marxist, classicist, Romantic or existentialist. The queries cut across all such *topoi*. De Man was indeed concerned with Romanticism but as an example of how in a given epoch any such ideology exposes anterior premises. At a different level Jean Starobinski examines Rousseau's appeal for liberation. The drama of revolt is cast in complete irreality. The authorial "I" of the text (Rousseau) is represented not only as omniscient but as virtue incarnate. Those addressed are idealized as pure victims of the tyrannies of society, blameless and shackled. This theatrical staging of the complex issues of human community and justice exhibits the seductions of rhetoric. Readers of any text may well be forewarned against the operations in them of conscious and unconscious motifs which flatter their self-esteem, sanction their desires or legitimize their power.

Current strategies of literary criticism are adept in unveiling all such intrusions and programmed influences in a writing. The field is especially wide open in our time when the cleavage of word and world is so generally accepted or even prized. Free course is accorded to invention, fabulation, oneirics, Gnosticism. With this loss of grounding criticism finds itself confined to textual, linguistic and rhetorical analysis, or deconstruction continues the critique of ideology so well exemplified in the case of Romanticism, yet in either case without final norms.

We are brought back, therefore, to the problem of word and world, of how words function, and whether we can have any confidence in our naming, imaging and predicating. Here we are further pushed back to the theory of signs. If signs are, indeed, arbitrary as regards what they signify, certainly a basic indeterminacy inheres in language. One can well recognize that the vocable "tree" used to designate an object, tree, is arbitrary as a matter of choice, not of necessity. So also with images. But this characterization of signifiers overlooks the whole basis and purpose of signifying which is to orient ourselves in reality and to get a *grip* on it. This intentionality pervades language and establishes meaning in its predication and rhetorics.

What is at stake here—granted the instability of language—is the urgency of speech and communication. This basic drive to establish meaning underlies all signifying and discourse. This urgency relates to the "force" of words not only in the sense of their meaning but that of their power and fatefulness. This suggests a test of all writings, a test which can be called phenomenological—a test not as to their structure, field of vision or ideology but as to their ultimate motivation.

It is at this point that the theologian cannot but appeal to the functioning of the word in the Scriptures of Israel. Naming is here rooted in the creation itself. God names what he creates. He calls by name those who are to carry out his purposes. To our first progenitor, Adam, is assigned the prerogative of naming the creatures. The story of the confusion of tongues at the Tower of Babel highlights the ordering function of speech. Israel's prophets identify the proclamations of Baal and the idolaters as "nothings" and delusions.

This grounding of the word in creation, law and covenant offers at least by analogy a criterion by which to assess the rich luxuriance of language in many cultures and in our own. Whether it is a question of images or stories, mythologies or social dreams, epiphanies, captivations or obsessions, a link with *realia* can be sought, both with those of our creaturely somatic givens and those of our empirical historical existence. This bonding of word and world not only safeguards us from gratuitous excursions into the inane but mediates to us the inexhaustible creativities of life itself.

That critical activity which we have called "theology and literature" has never properly represented a heresy-hunting program or even an exercise in Christian "apologetics" in the dogmatic sense. It has indeed sought to make place for the biblical heritage in the confluence of traditions which have fertilized our culture. The baffling interplay of motifs associated with aesthetic and spiritual syncretism has always been fascinating, going back especially to the merger of biblical and Hellenic components in the early Christian writings.

Prior to theological formulation Israel's ancient covenants determined a unique depth, vigor, realism and expectation in all that had to do with daily life and historical experience. This rich tissue of moral apperceptions lent a special substance and savor to existence and provided a more grounded kind of society than that of the Greek *polis*. The interweaving of these great and fateful strains and their vicissitudes can be traced through the centuries and down to our own time.

In the cultural disorder of today the biblical legacy may well serve as an illuminating test especially as regards contemporary Gnosticism and certain aspects of post-modernism. Indeed, the current resort in some quarters to contradiction, paradox and enigma is but a reflex which borrows its force from and is a tribute to the norms which it rejects. The appeal to some occult "other" or arcane erotics betrays a revulsion against the bonds of our human condition. But this is only to ignore the veritable plenitude, the heights and depths, the mystery of our creaturely pilgrimage as evoked in the annals of Scripture.

PART TWO

REMINISCENCES OF A CHANGING DISCIPLINE

4

New Testament Studies, 1920–1950

My earliest encounter with biblical studies at the seminary level takes me back to an unlikely place, the old Huguenot center of Montauban in the south of France. Here in the spring of 1919, while still in the uniform of a corporal in the U.S. Army, with four other American soldiers, I was a student at the Faculté Protestante de Théologie which moved the following year to Montpellier. All of us had been assigned to the Army School Detachment at the University of Toulouse in February. As pretheological students we were allowed to

In a tribute of the kind represented by this collection of papers some review of the vicissitudes of New Testament studies should be fitting even if it recalls only indirectly the immediate context in which Norman Perrin made his own invaluable contribution. Rather than a monograph on our discipline or a particular assessment of Norman's role in it the editors have encouraged my own diffident proposal: a senior colleague's reminiscences going back over half a century. These recollections, however personal and fortuitous, of earlier scholars and the climate of their labors both at home and abroad, even though confined to a period of three decades, may serve as an act of piety toward our predecessors and illumine our antecedents.

Viewed in this light as notes and soundings in a kind of family history, I trust I shall be excused for the inevitable personal reference, for the eclectic character of the memories and observations, which sometimes lead beyond our immediate discipline, and for the informal and anecdotal aspects of the review. When scholars foregather their interchanges are not always confined to their *Fach*. The household of learning has its own convivial occasions and its own oral tradition. The annals of our societies evoke not only monographs and journals but many delightful personalia. Grammarians are also human. In all such nonacademic interludes and exchanges Norman Perrin was no less robust a protagonist than on more formal occasions.—A.N.W.

This chapter originally appeared as "New Testament Studies, 1920-1950: Reminiscences of a Changing Discipline," in *The Journal of Religion* 64 (Oct. 1984), copyright 1984 by the University of Chicago. Published by the University of Chicago Press. Used by permission.

study at Montauban, whose dean was the great Calvin scholar, Émile Doumergue.

This seminary had celebrated its tercentenary in 1901. In 1919, after the end of the war, there were only a dozen French students, most of whom had just emerged from years of military service. Doumergue had a special class for our American group. In these months of the Versailles Peace Conference he was especially proud of the fact that Woodrow Wilson was a Presbyterian, a son of the manse, and that Geneva had been chosen as the site of the League of Nations and that its instrument was to be called a "covenant."

If I expand somewhat on this experience of a French seminary and its curriculum it will be in the interest of the cultural setting of biblical studies. As the church has many mansions so the household of learning has had many hearths, each with their special determinations. This matter of local differences and varying antecedents came home to me with particular force when at a later time, in connection with a visit to Rome, Oscar Cullmann—besides introductions to such New Testament scholars as Père S. Lyonnet at the Pontifical Biblical Institute and Père Augustino Mayer at the International College of S. Anselmo and Father Kirschbaum at the Gregorian University— gave me a letter to Professor Vittorio Subilia,[1] head of the Waldensian Theological Seminary who talked about the special history of his people and school and gave me a copy of his recent volume, *Gesù*.[2] Here as in the case of the Huguenot-founded Montauban was a school with an embattled past. To extend the typology I was later to recognize the interesting differences between the three chief centers of French Protestant learning: Montauban-Montpellier, Paris and Strassburg.

The character of biblical and other instruction at Montauban in 1919 is documented for me by my large notebook which includes notes on twelve courses. To supplement this I wrote recently to the

---

1. At the same time I delivered a box of candy sent by me to Signoria Subilia by that sister of Cullmann whom many will remember as the gracious hostess of his student hostel at Basel. Cullmann's services to Protestant-Catholic relations at a critical stage, and not only at the scholarly level, are well known, but his relations in Rome were not confined to Catholics. Another scholar who had close relations with the Waldensians was Walter Lowrie whom I shall mention below.

2. *Gesù nella più antica tradizione cristiana* (Torre Pellice, Italy: Editrice Claudiana, 1954).

Faculté at Montpellier through our New Testament colleague there, Professor Michel Bouttier. I was specially pleased to receive the answers to my questions from the librarian of the seminary, Mme. Preiss, because she was evidently the widow of the former distinguished New Testament scholar, Théo Preiss, with whom I had shared in the biblical study periods at the World Conference of Christian Youth at Amsterdam in 1939.

In his lectures on the New Testament at Montauban in 1919 Prof. André Arnal (1871–1943), dealing with the Book of Acts and the Apocalypse, related his discussion to German scholarship from Baur to Harnack, but showed his independence. Against Harnack he argued that Acts was written well after the death of Paul, and also held that the author intended a third writing. In the case of the Apocalypse Arnal attributed the original work to a Jew, but argued that a Christian redactor—indeed, John the Elder, but not to be confused with the author of the Fourth Gospel—had worked up the Jewish apocalypse about the year A.D. 100 for the churches of Asia Minor. Mme. Preiss informs me that Arnal's prior interest was dogmatics, to which he returned in 1924, being succeeded by that hardy perennial, a friend of many of us, Henri Clavier. But this is enough to suggest the scholarly climate of the seminary. It was Arnal who in 1926 revived its notable journal, *Études Théologiques et Religieuses*.

Significant also for New Testament study at the time was the course in Christology by Henri Bois who often cited Jülicher, Holtzmann, Wrede and Schmiedel in his study of the Gospels. Like later Montpellier teachers, such as Pierre Maury and Théo Preiss, Bois had wide ecumenical influence, especially in his case on the Student Christian Movement.

In retrospect it is of interest to me to be reminded that both the "social Gospel" and the new psychology were represented in that curriculum. Léon Maury, the father of Pierre Maury, taught a course on "Marx and Socialism," in which he dealt with current issues in French society including labor, unemployment and public welfare. Those who remember the later ecumenical discussions of social ethics in the "Life and Work" assemblies will recall that concern for the poor was strongly represented in some French Protestant circles even at the time when neo-orthodoxy was in the ascendant. My notes from the Montauban days remind me of one of our fellow students just demobilized at the age of twenty-five who initiated a weekly Protestant paper, *Le Soc* (The Ploughshare), aimed at peasants and industrial workers, "to counteract the propaganda that 'Protestantism is the religion of the bourgeoisie.' "

Louis Perrier who had degrees in both theology and medicine lectured on psychiatry, mental illness, criminality and drugs. Three years later at Oxford I found that this same area had emerged in theological and even biblical studies. At Mansfield College C.H. Dodd and the younger Micklem were introducing the new psychology into the study of the Gospels.

If I have dwelt too long on the Montauban experience it is to suggest the diversity and wider bearings of biblical study in our period. In a much later letter that admired poet-scholar Ernst Fuchs who meant so much to Norman Perrin and myself scolded me for spending part of a sabbatical at Basel (and by implication the other part at Strassburg) where "they may understand something about our German questions but very little of our German answers." But perhaps the post-Bultmannian questions and answers could be better understood at some remove, and perhaps there were other questions also deserving of attention.

Since my first two years of formal theological study were at Mansfield College in Oxford 1921–23 I shared to that extent in the English context of Norman Perrin's later study. In that period the only university chair in theology in England open to non-Anglicans was the Rylands professorship at Manchester held in Norman's time by T.W. Manson, who had been preceded by my own teacher, C.H. Dodd, and before that by another Congregationalist, A.S. Peake. It was only in my time at Oxford that higher degrees in divinity were opened to Dissenters. Even a great scholar like James Moffatt who had succeeded Alexander Souter at Mansfield in 1915, and who was followed there by Dodd, could find a suitable chair only in Scotland. It is not surprising that nonconformist scholars, like Norman himself later, should be attracted by offers from the United States. About the time that Moffatt went to Union Theological Seminary in New York and Nathaniel Micklem to Kingston in Canada, Yale almost persuaded Dodd to take the place of Bacon at his retirement in 1928.

When I enrolled in Dodd's classes at Mansfield College in 1921 he was in his thirty-eighth year. He had taken two firsts at Oxford, had

had Souter and George Buchanan Gray as his teachers in Scripture at Mansfield, and had been profoundly impressed by Harnack at Berlin in 1907. Like B.H. Streeter and A.E.J. Rawlingson he had been a member of William Sanday's notable seminar on New Testament Studies, and was now participating in the influential labors of that group headed by Streeter concerned with Synoptic studies. Streeter's *Four Gospels* was published in 1924.[3]

The recent thorough and delightful life of Dodd by Frederick Dillistone well characterizes his appearance in the early twenties.[4] Walking beside his colleague, Vernon Bartlet, the church historian, whom the students saw as an "elongated saint," Dillistone remembers the pair as "giraffe" and "robin." "Dodd was tiny in comparison, quick in his movements, a face alert without strain, a well-proportioned head with dark slightly wavy hair—he seemed almost to hop and dance by the side of his venerable colleague."[5]

I have a small yellow notebook reporting Dodd's lectures that year for two terms: "The Teaching of Jesus according to Tradition Common to Matthew and Luke," and "Synoptic Data for the Life of Jesus." The notes evidence his training in classics, his acquaintance with the authorities of the time, his disagreements with Albert Schweitzer, anticipations of "realized eschatology," that concern with translation into common experience which marked his then-recent first important book, *The Meaning of Paul for Today*,[6] and his interest in the new psychology. Dodd, as Dillistone tells us, was at that time going through a difficult personal crisis, and that same impact of psychiatric investigation which at this time touched the university, including Streeter's circle, also provided him with persuasive insights into the early Christian experience and records.

In February of that year Albert Schweitzer came to give the Dale Lectures on Civilization and Ethics at Mansfield College. At this period Schweitzer was raising money by his organ concerts to restore his hospital and further his work at Lambaréné after his enforced

3. B.H. Streeter, *The Four Gospels: A Study of Origins* (London: Macmillan & Co., 1924).
4. *C.H. Dodd: Interpreter of the New Testament* (Grand Rapids: Wm. B. Eerdmans, 1977).
5. Ibid., 10.
6. (London: Allen & Unwin, 1920; reprint, New York: Meridian, 1957).

absence during World War I. Since I knew French I served as a kind of amanuensis to him with his correspondence. The Schweitzers had a room in the home of the college principal, Dr. Selbie. The great doctor worked incessantly at irregular hours. He was a massive figure, and Mrs. Selbie plaintively admitted that even his step or a clearing of the throat at 3 A.M. could shake the house! His correspondence had mostly to do with his organ concerts in various English cathedrals. In Oxford I showed him the way to the two organs on which he played; those at New College and Christ Church.

I myself had become particularly interested in Schweitzer's views of Jesus' teaching, especially through Walter Lowrie of Rome. Lowrie had translated a part of Schweitzer's earlier Strassburg thesis, *Das Abendmal* (1901), that part which Lowrie entitled, *The Mystery of the Kingdom of God*, and published in 1913.[7] This earlier work of Schweitzer helps to clarify his views of Jesus' eschatology so much condensed in the last two chapters of *The Quest of the Historical Jesus*. *The Quest* in its German original in 1906 had at first been enthusiastically appraised in England by Sanday.[8] But Sanday later retracted his support of Schweitzer's position following the publication of the English translation in 1910, and his coolness to it was reinforced among English scholars by the lectures given at Oxford in 1909 by Ernst von Dobschütz and published the following year under the title, *The Eschatology of the Gospels*.[9]

C.H. Dodd in the lectures I heard in 1921–22 reflected this disagreement with Schweitzer. Where the latter held that Jesus in the last phase of his ministry deliberately committed himself to death as one who would alone and "for many" suffer the Messianic tribula-

---

7. Walter Lowrie (1868–1959), Rector of St. Paul's American Church in Rome from 1907 until 1930, was a pioneer in introducing to English-speaking readers first Schweitzer, then Barth, and above all Kierkegaard. I first met him at Rome in 1920 and heard him preach the Christmas sermon on which he based his little book, *The Birth of the Divine Child* (New York, London: Longmans, Green, & Co., 1926). Lowrie, who had studied at Princeton and at the American Academy in Rome, had earlier written on early Christian art (*Monuments of the Early Church* [New York: Macmillan Co., 1901]), was an idiosyncratic genius who shared something of Schweitzer's imaginative power in transcending academic categories. In teaching the life of Jesus later I always found his *Jesus According to St. Mark* (New York, London: Longmans, Green, & Co., 1929), based on Schweitzer's thoroughgoing eschatology, an indispensable text. I have lately been glad to hear that a life of Lowrie is now in preparation by Donald H. Fox.

8. William Sanday, *The Life of Christ in Recent Research* (Oxford: Clarendon Press, 1907), 77–89, esp. 88.

9. (London: Hodder & Stoughton, 1910).

tion and birth-throes of the Kingdom, Dodd held that this challenge to God was in direct contradiction to Jesus' outlook as indicated in the second trial of the temptation narrative. Dodd also, with others, queried the confidence with which Schweitzer took over Matthew 10 as historical. But with much British scholarship Dodd was unable to grasp the radically alien outlook of Jesus as Schweitzer, Tyrrell and Loisy were able to do or the scale of conception which distinguished Schweitzer from all others including Johannes Weiss. The vitality of Dodd's contributions throughout his career went back to his Welsh pietism, including his openness to psychological and other nondogmatic dimensions of the religious life. Congenial to this was also that Platonism which surfaced especially in his "realized eschatology" and his interest in the Fourth Gospel. For the wider public of his time such books of his as *The Authority of the Bible* and the *Romans* in the Moffatt series represented a great clarification.[10] But the scholarly fraternity will remember him especially for his share in the accumulating expertise of his period.

One anecdote of these Mansfield days is appropriate here. At the annual party given for the faculty in the Junior Common Room students of that time like John Whale were accorded a certain license at the expense of their elders. In the spring of 1922 the American J. Edgar Park, later president of Wheaton College, was on a sabbatical in Oxford and attending lectures at Mansfield. He was very popular with the whole community, as those who remember his wit and grace can appreciate. Honored as the last speaker Park closed his oratory with a vision of being taken up to heaven in the hereafter. There to his astonishment he found Vernon Bartlet "instructing the Church Fathers as to where they went wrong, and Charles Harold Dodd telling the Apostles what they really meant."[11]

10. C.H. Dodd, *The Authority of the Bible* (London: Nisbet & Co., 1928); and *The Epistle of Paul to the Romans* (London: William Collins Sons, 1932).

11. Teaching at this time in Oxford were also Streeter, whom I have mentioned, C.W. Emmet and R.H. Lightfoot. The latter, whose lectures on the theology of the Gospels had more the character of meditation than analysis, gave then no indication so far as I can recall of his subsequent interest in form-criticism or in the ideas of Lohmeyer which later so attracted him. Of visitors to Oxford at that period besides Schweitzer the most memorable as touching our field was T.R. Glover of Cambridge, known first of all as a classicist, but whose book on Jesus had an immense influence. I had Glover later at Yale. He never brought anything to class but a Greek Testament and concordance.

Fifty-five years before the time of this writing, in 1923, I entered on my last year of B.D. study, now at the Yale Divinity School at its old location on Elm Street in New Haven. So I found myself in the classes of Benjamin W. Bacon and Frank Porter, as well as of Bainton, Calhoun and Weigle. With undergraduates some of us had a course with Rostovtzeff. Like myself Erwin Goodenough had come from Oxford, where I had known him at Lincoln College, and was soon to be teaching in several departments. I was paying my bills by teaching French half-time to freshmen, an area of fieldwork looked on as suspect for a theologue among some of my fellow students.

This is not the place to rehearse Bacon's career and contributions. Roy Harrisville in his invaluable book on him in the Society of Biblical Literature series Studies in American Biblical Scholarship has excellently characterized his learning, his foci of investigation, his methods and the influences which determined him.[12] In an unpublished review of that book I have stressed the Puritan strain in his piety which entered into combination with his Hegelianism. Bacon's chapel services, of which I still have notes, were memorable. No doubt "religious experience" was the telltale center not only of theological liberalism but of its biblical interpretation in this period. But religious experience, whether Platonic as with Dodd, or Hegelian as with Bacon, could be anchored in the Incarnation as it was by Dodd, or in the Atonement as it was by Bacon.

This suggests another similarity between Dodd and Bacon. In evoking the pages of the Gospels they could both appeal to common human experience and extrabiblical analogies. At one point when Dodd was discussing the great throngs that sought out Jesus in the Galilean ministry, he stopped and cited the headlines of the day: the immense mass movement of the multitudes in India which by a profound impulse gathered about Gandhi and impeded his movements. Bacon, in an effort to convey the extravagant power of faith in the early church, found an analogy in the figure of Jeanne d'Arc, because, he wrote, "I feel the need of some career within the control of modern research." So he cites the points of comparison: the lowly origin,

---

12. Roy A. Harrisville, *Benjamin Wiser Bacon, Pioneer in American Biblical Criticism*, Studies in American Biblical Scholarship 2 (Missoula, Mont.: Scholars Press, 1976).

the unschooled appeal, the sway over the imaginations and loyalties of the lowly, the shrewd strictures on the doctors and prelates of the day, the native authority of truth in debate, the legendary character of the yet actual deeds, the short careers of a year or more, the death compassed through religious jealousy, and the moving detail that the heroine was summoned to her task by the title *fille Dé*.[13] Bacon was not ignoring the disproportion between the two instances, but was intent in his way on the basic dynamics of revelation and of history.

If Bacon did not anticipate form-criticism in the strict sense yet his focus was constantly on the determination of the tradition by the interests of the early communities, especially liturgical. He underestimated the importance of early Christian eschatology,[14] but he was very persuasive in dealing with what he called Christian midrash and poetic symbolism in the texts. His seminars, like his books on Matthew and John, were so dense with reference and had so many facets that the student was at once dismayed and excited. It was this laboratory character of his pursuits as well as his sense of ministry which more than anything else led me to New Testament studies after a period in the pastorate.

As compared with the robust Bacon who as an undergraduate football player had been called "freight-train" Bacon, Porter was a gentle soul. But as "Roly" Bainton wrote in a review of Harrisville's book on Porter and with reference to the latter's portrait in the Common Room of the Divinity School, "that bald little fellow with the celluloid collar and string tie was also one of those early luminaries who put to flight armies of aliens."[15] Nor should his portentous wife Delia be forgotten, Dorcas of all good works in the school and in New Haven, a veritable "mother-in-Israel." At one of the all-school parties and stunt nights the students had primed a policeman to collar Professor Porter as he viewed the festivities. The expected reaction of Delia took place. She flew across the floor and pushed the officer of the law aside, exclaiming, "You leave my husband alone!"

---

13. *Jesus, Son of God* (New York: Henry Holt & Co., 1930), 40.
14. My B.D. thesis echoing Schweitzer's insights came back approved by Bacon, the sole reader, with no notes or comments whatever except the concluding signature, "B.W. Bacon."
15. *Reflection* [Yale Divinity School] 75 (Jan. 1978):12.

In the summer of 1924 following my graduation from the Divinity School I had an opportunity to go to Berlin, and Bacon gave me a letter of introduction to Adolf Deissmann. Thus I was able to visit his famous *en Christō* seminar. This now recalls to me the wide discussions of those days of the "mysticism" of Paul, to which Schweitzer added his contribution in a book with that title. Deissmann also introduced me to one of his students. By way of helping me with my German we read together the new edition of Deissmann's *Paulus*.[16] This work based on the author's *koine* studies (like the studies by Sir William Ramsay with their attention to the topography, roads and cities of Paul's mission) sought to place the apostle in his setting, and its focus was very different from that of Porter's *The Mind of Christ in Paul*.[17] All such investigations with their diverse *topoi*, tools and approaches, with the stir they occasioned in scholarly circles, seem today to belong to another world. But the disciplined wrestle with the past was transmitted to new generations, and tested findings taken up into our later agenda.

During my visit to Berlin I was fortunate to hear two lectures of a course on the Church Fathers by Harnack, near the close of his career. Though I was ill-prepared to recognize the grasp of his treatment I treasure this glimpse of the master, as in a totally different realm I cherish the memory of William Butler Yeats, seen only once as he was striding near the banks of the Cherwell in Oxford.

These first experiences of a lecture in an eighteenth-century *Horsaal* or *Aula* of a German university had their surprises. If not "the last enchantments" at least the last simulacra of the Middle Ages hung over the ritual. One must picture the setting: the high ceiling, the high windows, the elevated podium and desk, the amphitheater of narrow benches often rising steeply, the students gathering at the gong and awaiting the entrance of Harnack or Lietzmann or Deissmann. Wilhelm Pauck at Chicago, who had known this period in Berlin, used to be called on by his students at convivial occasions for his inimitable rehearsal of this little drama. Commotion at the door would signal the arrival of the professor. The students would

16. A. Deissmann, *Paulus: Eine kultur-und religionsgeschichtliche Skizze*, 2d rev. ed. (Tübingen: J.C.B. Mohr [Paul Siebeck], 1925).
17. (New York, London: Charles Scribner's Sons, 1930).

rise. First would appear an *Assistent* bowed over with a great pile of lexicons and texts, the Wagner or *famulus* of Goethe's Faust, then a number of *Dozenten*, and finally there would occur the epiphany of the *Magister* himself. At his sign the students would be seated and the lecture would be opened with the words *Meine Damen und Herrn*.

When I returned to Yale in the fall of 1928 for doctoral study Carl Kraeling had followed Bacon. He had published his Columbia dissertation, *Anthropos and Son of Man*, had given lectures at Yale on form-criticism and was one of the first in this country along with B.S. Easton and Frederick Grant to introduce the European work in this area.[18] J.Y. Campbell of Scotland, later at Cambridge with Dodd, was also teaching at Yale.

These names to which that of C.C. Torrey should be added suggest a number of recollections some of which belong to a somewhat later time. Torrey had a course on Aramaic in the Fourth Gospel which would have been very sparsely attended if he had not admitted some like myself who had had no Aramaic. He gave us a dozen touchstones by which we could recognize Semiticisms and then Aramaicisms in John's Greek. It was not long after this period that the notorious clashes occurred at meetings of the Society of Biblical Literature between Torrey on the one hand and Goodspeed and Riddle on the other over Torrey's views on the Aramaic origins of a number of the New Testament writings. Torrey, slight in stature but acid in debate, could be very peremptory in refusing further discussion with those who, he averred, knew only one of the two languages in question. After one of these jousts which I was unable to attend an observer reported to me that of the three protagonists the society could recognize two scholars and one gentleman. Since Goodspeed was undoubtedly always the gentleman that leaves only one category undecided.

In the discussions of Dodd's "realized eschatology" which was first broached in this scholar's Shaffer Lectures on the parables at Yale in 1935 it will be remembered that J.Y. Campbell and Kenneth Clark published important papers challenging Dodd's interpretation of the crucial verbs *engiken* and *ephthasen* (the Kingdom has *drawn near*; the

---

18. C. Kraeling, *Anthropos and Son of Man: A Study in the Religious Syncretism of the Hellenistic Orient* (New York: Columbia University Press, 1927).

Kingdom has *come upon* us).[19] This is going a little ahead of my story but I mention it because of Campbell who was of great assistance to me in the writing of my doctoral thesis.

The committee for my projected dissertation on eschatology and ethics in the teaching of Jesus included Kraeling, Campbell and Erwin Goodenough. Since I had completed residence requirements at Yale it was agreed that I could well get the benefit of study at Harvard and especially suggestions from Kirsopp Lake in the further defining of my topic. Anyone working in the line of Schweitzer was at this time under some handicaps. I have under my eyes as I write a letter from Walter Lowrie in September of 1929 just as I was settling into Divinity Hall at Cambridge. Lowrie had had disappointments with the reception of his book on Mark (1929) and the reprinting of his translation of Schweitzer's *Skizze* (*The Mystery of the Kingdom of God* [1925]).[20] Lowrie wrote:

> For myself I have serious counsel to give you. If you would have long life and would see good days, keep mum on the subject of eschatology. It will be better if you do not read my book on St. Mark. I am afraid our conversations at Babbio may reillumine your interest in a subject which is highly dangerous in these days. Your teachers give you good advice: eschatology is a subject which the good and the great conspire to shun.

I had an interview with Kirsopp Lake and A.D. Nock the day after my arrival at Harvard and the upshot rather tended to confirm Lowrie's forebodings. Lake observed that I could deal with Jesus' eschatology but that I would just come out with another theory about it. One could discuss the data but there were not enough data to reach a conclusion. But then he listed certain problems that merited discussion, such as the relation of the church to eschatological salvation. This he illustrated by a little joke of his own. "Am I saved?" It all depends on whether one reads the present, *sozomenos*, or the

---

19. In a recent letter Millar Burrows recalls Dodd's lectures given during Burrow's first year on the Divinity School faculty at Yale. "They were my first encounter with realized eschatology. I remember a discussion meeting with Dodd in which I pointed out to him a fact about the Syriac rendering of *ēngiken* and *ephthasen* which he used in his book to prove the opposite of what I took it to prove. (Later I cited the facts in an SBL paper, never published, which Cadbury said demolished the last possible support of Dodd's position!) The lectures impressed me, but didn't convince me."

20. (London: A. & C. Black, 1925; 1st ed., 1914).

perfect, *sesōsmenos*! In recommending a book of Windisch to me he threw in the remark that for the chair at Leyden he had recommended Windisch and not von Dobschütz, adding a little maliciously *ein Liberal und kein Preusse.*

I remember one social occasion with Lake when he told stories about Oxford and Leyden. A student at Leyden was being examined in Scripture by four members of the faculty. Seeing that he was very nervous it was suggested to him that he himself select a passage to be explored. Even now the young man was at a loss until, evidently, certain verses had occurred to him only to be rejected. He explained that the passage he had thought of would not be appropriate. What was that passage? "I saw in my vision, and behold four great beasts. . ." (Dan. 7:2–3).

Lake later wisely steered me into limiting myself to the Gospel of Matthew, but within this compass I was encouraged to go on with my study of eschatology and ethics. After a time he left Cambridge temporarily and the patrician James Hardy Ropes took over the role of counselor while I took everything that Nock offered in this his first year at Harvard. George Foot Moore had retired and Cadbury was to return only after the retirement of Ropes.

A retrospect of this kind inevitably draws attention to the variety of specializations, tools, methods and approaches contributing to our common field. Across the broad front of Christian beginnings differing thrusts and areas of investigation are pursued by individual workers, sometimes in a line of succession with their teachers and sometimes in a team effort. Sometimes the focus or direction is determined by the ethos of a particular institution or of a "school" as in the case of Chicago.

I can illustrate by reference to the situation at Harvard in the twenties and thirties. In memorializing Henry Cadbury at a later time I could not but note that in his work on Acts and his main attention to Hellenistic studies he had been drawn into a line there which ran from La Piana and Kirsopp Lake to Ropes and Nock.[21] Lake had enlisted him as early as 1919 in the team effort of *The*

---

21. "In Memoriam: Henry Joel Cadbury, 1883–1974," *New Testament Studies* 21 (1974–75):313–17.

Beginnings of Christianity.[22] In any case the main focus at Harvard was for long on Greek Hellenistic studies. Skeptics have been known to wonder whether in those years the New Testament specialists knew any Hebrew. Perhaps they left all that to George Foot Moore. At one time the English department asked Lake and Ropes to teach the usual course for undergraduates on the Bible as literature. Lake is quoted as saying that he would like to take over the Old Testament part of the course since he knew little about it.

My point is not to disparage the great line of teachers at Harvard but to illustrate the diversity of labors in our different centers. In this same period—as with Harper's earlier initiative at Chicago—teaching and scholarship at Union Theological Seminary and at Yale were more church-oriented. Those Scotchmen and churchmen who taught at Union, Moffatt, E.F. Scott, Frame and Foakes-Jackson, taught both "Introduction" and piety, and with great learning. Yale carried on a tradition in which the Semitic backgrounds of the New Testament were constantly in view: witness C.C. Torrey, Frank Porter, Millar Burrows, and Bacon himself who had begun his career with Pentateuchal studies.

Apart from the factor of institutional variety it can be illuminating, and need not be intrusive, to note the variety of personal religious commitments of workers in our field in relation to their careers and contributions. No doubt the common canons of scholarly method were shared by all our great predecessors but their particular private or confessional orientation could be reflected in their labors and agenda. Apart from such main distinctions as those between our Jewish and Christian colleagues, or Protestant and Catholic, or "liberal" and "evangelical," one can recall the special impact of neo-orthodoxy at one period on certain aspects of our studies.

An intriguing case in point for such special motivation would be that again of Henry Cadbury the Quaker, secretary of the Society of Biblical Literature from 1916 to 1933, and of the American Schools for Oriental Research from 1934 to 1954. No one would have accused Henry of a parochial standpoint. But neither can one deny that the vigor and Socratic method of his teaching, his costly testimony for

---

22. Full title: *The Beginnings of Christianity: Part I The Acts of the Apostles*, ed. F.J. Foakes-Jackson and Kirsopp Lake, 5 vols. (London: Macmillan & Co., 1920–33).

academic freedom, and the nondogmatic empiricism of such writings as *The Peril of Modernizing Jesus* traced to his membership in the Society of Friends, whose representative he was at the award of the Nobel Peace Prize at Oslo in 1947.[23] Henry Cadbury had his convictions and his scruple, and these both animated a lifetime of learning, also in Quaker studies. It is amusing that his scruple could once have led E.J. Goodspeed in the sequel to a discussion in the RSV Committee to say of him that "the consciousness of even a single certainty would be an insupportable weight upon his mind."

For another kind of personal orientation related to distinguished achievement one can take the case of Erwin Goodenough whom, as noted, I knew from his student days at Oxford. As a rebel against an early pietistic nurture the ethos of Yale—carrying on in new ways the New England tradition tracing to Jonathan Edwards—was understandably uncongenial to him. Teaching in the three fields of classics, history and religion he was always restive in his relations with the Divinity School and he felt that the delays in his promotion were related to the independence of his personal views and teaching. At his last lecture which drew a large attendance of admiring students he let go with a blast against what he saw as the reigning conformity and pietism of the institution. There had been an earlier *deboire* in which the Roman Catholic chaplain had carried on for a year or two a protest against Erwin's presentation of the beginnings of the church in his popular course in European history. Morton Smith in his authoritative and balanced review of Goodenough's work on Jewish symbols speaks of "the religion of conformity and respectability with which [Goodenough] collided at Yale."[24] Smith's assessment of this great scholar ends with the tribute that though he misconstrued much of his material yet "like Columbus he revealed a new world."

I have gone into this special case because it highlights some of the deeper tensions and motivations which have always accompanied our studies. Scholars have been divided not only as they appealed to a secular or a devout tradition, but also to this or that confessional heritage. One recalls Ernst Käsemann's repudiation in the name of

---

23. *The Peril of Modernizing Jesus* (New York: Macmillan Co., 1937).

24. "Goodenough's *Jewish Symbols* in Retrospect," *Journal of Biblical Literature* 86 (1967):63.

the "German university tradition" of pressure to "clericalize and confessionalize theological study" in Germany after World War II. He saw reformers of curriculum and method as substituting edification and indoctrination for that radicalism of inquiry in which "everything is put in question." Animated by concern for the disorientation of the students at the time, the authorities were turning the seminaries into *Fachschule*.[25]

I need only add to this excursus on the various commitments of our colleagues or of their institutions or traditions that wisdom is finally justified both by her works and by her children. If, indeed, there are impediments or obliquities here or there in the search for truth these are not confined to the households of faith. One might even ask whether either our texts or our traditions of learning would have survived apart from these ancient pieties.

In the thirties and forties the annual meetings of the Society of Biblical Literature continued to take place during the Christmas holidays at Union Theological Seminary in New York. Some papers would be read to the whole body but separate sessions were the rule for the New Testament and Old Testament scholars. When a tyro read his first paper in the former group it was something of an ordeal. Flanked by the president of the Society or some other veteran, he looked down from the platform on Cadbury, Enslin, Goodenough, Nock and McCasland who usually sat in the first row and made the first comments. Somewhere nearby would be W.H.P. Hatch, the text critic, Kirsopp Lake, F.C. Grant, B.W. Bacon, E.J. Goodspeed, C.C. McCown, S.C. Case, Floyd Filson and others. In 1930 the fiftieth anniversary of the society was celebrated. A memorial address was delivered by Nathaniel Schmidt of Cornell, and reminiscences were read by D.G. Lyon of Harvard, Cyrus Adler of Dropsie, C.C. Torrey of Yale, George A. Barton of the University of Pennsylvania and by Cadbury.

To evoke further the activities of this period in our field I can turn to Chicago where I joined the Federated Theological Faculty of the University at the time of its inauguration in 1943. This is all the more appropriate since it bears on the setting into which Norman Perrin entered when he joined the Divinity School faculty in 1964. In 1943

---

25. "Kritik eines Reformvorschlags," *Evangelische Theologie* 12 (1952):245–49.

the Harper tradition of concern for extension services beyond the campus to the laity still had its echoes. I took over a kind of great-books course from Ernest Colwell which included writings from the Bible and the early Fathers and which was open to any registrants. Papers were still coming in occasionally from all over the Middle West from students enrolled in correspondence courses, the syllabi for which had been prepared long since by such scholars as Burton and Votaw.

Colwell himself was carrying on an old tradition of Goodspeed. Once a week in the early morning a group of students and colleagues would gather at his home for manuscript studies and breakfast. In 1948 Goodspeed himself returned for a major colloquium on paleography which drew specialists from many centers including Dumbarton Oaks. Out of this consultation emerged the International Text Critical Project. These activities of course involved both Harold Willoughby and Allen Wikgren, as well as Merrill Parvis.

Willoughby, an otherworldly scholar-saint of the ancient mold who had somehow inherited from Winfred Garrison the most beautiful study in America—in the Disciples Divinity House—divided his time between illuminated manuscripts, hagiography of Chicago's earlier luminaries, especially Burton, and fostering care over both the students' New Testament Club (as old as the University) and the Chicago Society of Biblical Research. This society included not only our colleagues in the Oriental Institute like Ralph Marcus and Ray Bowman, but also scholars from all the Chicago seminaries: Garrett, Maywood, McCormick, Seabury-Western and others. A valuable index to the biblical agenda at Chicago in the forties as well as a monument to Willoughby's zeal is still to be found in the society's symposium which he edited, *The Study of the Bible Today and Tomorrow.*[26]

If one looks in this volume for evidence of the earlier "Chicago school" and its social-historical methodology one will find it clearly only in papers by F.C. Grant and C.C. McCown who at this time were no longer in the area. This tends to confirm the discussion of this "school" in Robert Funk's notable paper, "The Watershed of the American Biblical Tradition."[27] One should not conclude, however,

26. (Chicago: University of Chicago Press, 1947).
27. Full title: "The Watershed of the American Biblical Tradition: The Chicago School, First Phase, 1892–1920," *Journal of Biblical Literature* 95 (1976):4–22.

that the social science approach to the history of religion was repudiated at Chicago. In the forties members of the biblical faculty, old and new, had indeed their own special interests which were not those of such predecessors as Shailer Mathews, Case and Riddle.[28] The fertilizing input of the school could still be recognized indirectly not least in the allergy to the rising influence of neo-orthodoxy in this period. This sociological empiricism was also congenial to the important theological approach associated with H.N. Weiman and represented by Daniel Day Williams, Bernard M. Loomer and Bernard E. Meland in the Divinity School.

One further feature of New Testament studies at Chicago was our dual relation as scholars both to the Theological Faculty and to the Division of the Humanities in the University. As members of the Department of Early Christian Literature in that division doors were open to us for wide exchanges with workers in related fields. How important such contacts could be was evident subsequently in the case of Norman Perrin especially as regards the later developments of his thinking and method.

In concluding these reminiscences I gather up some experiences abroad when I taught as an exchange professor from Chicago at the University of Frankfurt in the spring of 1951 and the winter of 1952–53. Though I was teaching modern literature in the English Seminar yet I soon had opportunities to visit a number of theological faculties. In fact I had not been in Frankfurt very long before the Bultmanns invited me to Marburg for a Sunday dinner. Two weeks later Franklin Littell who was at the time attached to the religious section of the American Military Government in Frankfurt took me again to Marburg in a staff car where I spoke to Ernst Benz's seminar. Benz was just about to leave for Athens where he was joining the widely represented 1900th anniversary celebration of St. Paul's Mediterranean mission. Henri Clavier who was also on the vessel which retraced Paul's journeys by sea later remarked that they had omitted the shipwreck at the island of Malta.

---

28. When Allen Wikgren edited a volume in honor of Willoughby (*Early Christian Origins* [Chicago: Quadrangle Books, 1961]) the sociological approach was still evident especially in the papers by Carl Kraeling who had joined the Oriental Institute as director, Frederick Grant and Sherman Johnson. My own contribution was entitled, "Social Factors in Early Christian Eschatology."

My most interesting experience at Marburg, however, was in a subsequent visit (1958) when I spoke before the theological faculty and students on the New Testament theme of the struggle with "the principalities and powers," interpreting this "theologumenon" as offering the basis for a social ethic in the church. This was of course an impossible view for Bultmann who in his New Testament theology had identified the *archontes* and *kyriotētes* with such spiritual tyrants as sin and the flesh, only to be overcome by Christ himself "at the end."[29] But in the discussion after the presentation, W.G. Kümmel, who sat next to Bultmann in the front row and next to Eltester, took my side on one aspect of the matter, and I was glad to let them take up the remaining time.

Bultmann was always wonderfully gracious in all my contacts with him. He was constantly surprising me by his courtesies. After supper one evening in which Mrs. Wilder and I were both guests with his family he took me into his study. He wanted to speak about one of my brother's novels which he had read. He then pulled out a translation of a poem of Hölderlin which I had recently worked over, and commented on it. He also had at hand and made some points about a translation of the First Epistle of John which I had made, one in which I had indented as "poetry" those parallelisms which Bultmann had attributed to an earlier quasi-gnostic source.

It was in 1951 that the famous "trial" of Bultmann took place. It was not a matter of excommunicating him in any sense, but of removing him from some board of examiners in the Hesse-Nassau church jurisdiction. I happened to be present at one session of the proceedings. Representatives of what we would call the grass-roots churches felt that the great scholar's views were dangerous and subversive. Finally no less a figure than Martin Niemöller arose and carried the day against the opposition, arguing that the scholars of the church should not be trammeled in their own areas of service.

My Göttingen contacts in 1951 offered a double privilege: acquaintance with the great lexicographer Walter Bauer, and participation with many distinguished scholars—including some of Norman Perrin's later teachers here—in a remarkable consultation.

---

29. *Theology of the New Testament*, tran. K. Grobel (New York: Charles Scribner's Sons, 1951), I: 256–59.

For my meeting with Bauer I can do no better than reproduce the notes I made at the time.

> Supper at 7 with Walter Bauer and his wife—introduced by Wilbur Gingrich. Bauer showed me page proofs through *sigma* of the fourth edition of the great *Wörterbuch*, and galleys of the rest. Thousands of new references had been added to this edition [published the following year by Topelmann in Berlin], and a greater enrichment than between the second and third [1937] editions. The work held up eighteen months already. The printing being done in Leipzig and Berlin, and the shortage of paper and East Zone difficulties occasioning delay. . . .
>
> One son died in the War. He had just finished his studies in German and in English. The bereaved fiancée now married to a professor of American history at Columbia. One son a chemist in Germany. One daughter a teacher of art in the University of London and writing a book on Rembrandt.
>
> They are very fond of Gingrich who is seeing to a translation of the *Wörterbuch* for the University of Chicago Press.

Bauer had taken over the succession to Preuschen's earlier *Handwörterbuch* after the latter's death in 1920. In an article in *New Testament Studies*, after Bauer himself had died, Gingrich writes:

> Professor Bauer was not content to rest on his laurels with the successful completion of the third edition. He was acutely aware that there was a great reservoir of late Greek literature full of parallels to New Testament usage, which had never been systematically investigated. . . . One might have thought that his obligation to scholarship was discharged with the completion of the fourth edition, when he was seventy-five years of age. He had no such idea, and he pressed on with work on the fifth revised and greatly augmented edition before the fourth had finally come from the press.[30]

It was just at this moment that I was Bauer's guest, and my most vivid memory is the eagerness and pride with which he pointed to upper shelves in his study containing the files in progress of his material for that future edition.

When one recalls that he had suffered for some years from an eye infection and was compelled to use a magnifying glass for his reading one can further appreciate the sense I had of standing in the pres-

---

30. "The Contributions of Professor Walter Bauer to New Testament Lexicography," *New Testament Studies* 9 (1962–63):5, 8.

ence not only of a lovable but heroic scholar. It was, moreover, a special pleasure to me that when my little book, *Otherworldliness and the New Testament*, was published a few years later in Göttingen it was one of Bauer's daughters who did the translation.[31]

The Ecumenical Consultation in Göttingen in June 1951 to which I have referred had as its theme "Individual and Community," one among several topics which the Study Department of the World Council of Churches was exploring under the general head of "The Social and Political Message of the Bible Today." Among the thirty-three participants were such well-known New Testament scholars as Jeremias, Schneemelcher and Greeven. In Chicago I had been working with another regional group concerned with the same topic, chaired by George Ernest Wright and including Floyd Filson of McCormick, Holt Graham of Seabury-Western, E.P. Blair of Garrett, and Coert Rylaarsdam, J.L. Adams and J.H. Nichols of the Federated Theological Faculty. Some of our papers had been forwarded to the Göttingen meeting. Wright later edited the publication of our extended Chicago discussions under the title *The Biblical Doctrine of Man in Society*.[32]

It was of absorbing interest to hear the discussion at Göttingen at a time when the problem of society was still so acute after the Nazi period. It was evident that the biblical grounds for social order and especially the Lutheran political ethic needed to be radically rethought. Not only systematic theologians took part but also a jurist, an economist and other laymen.

The most outspoken contribution was made by H.J. Iwand of Göttingen who noted that after 1933 in Germany the Protestants, the Roman Catholics and the liberal elements were so far apart that they could not unite in opposition to Hitler, each defending their own prerogatives and not those of a common justice. Taking off from Karl Barth he held that it was the duty of the Christian to oppose the corruption of the state, and not to misread Luther's doctrine of the two realms in such a way as to encourage political abstention.

---

31. *Otherworldliness and the New Testament* (New York: Harper & Brothers, 1954); German translation, *Weltfremdes Christentum?* (Göttingen: Vandenhoeck & Ruprecht, 1958).
32. Ecumenical Biblical Studies 2 (London: SCM Press, 1954).

Yet, he observed, we lacked a casuistry when it came to refuting the errors of the German National Church.

What particularly interested me in the course of the meeting was that when the New Testament scholars made their reports there was very little that could further a clarification. For a bridge from the New Testament to modern social and political responsibilities we were offered only *agape* and the model of the primitive Christian community. The fear of admitting any human role in the work of God foreclosed any social programs. This same otherworldly spirituality dominated the formulation of "the Christian Hope," the theme of the Evanston Assembly of the World Council of Churches in 1954, on whose preparatory Committee of Twenty-Five I also served. The imminent eschatology of Jesus and his followers, the conception of the Kingdom as "idea" and not as "symbol"—to use Perrin's later distinction—ruled out any this-age social implications of the Gospel. Just how unstructured any moral theology could be was suggested by Jeremias's statement that the basis of social ethic in the New Testament is the forgiveness of sins.

Yet one significant input here came not from the biblical scholars but from Iwand who appealed to the Christus Victor theme in the New Testament, familiar in the work of Gustav Aulén. Citing H. Schlier and Erik Peterson, Iwand argued that the New Testament church evidenced a genuine political consciousness, even though symbolic and unformulated, in its confrontation with the empire. Its acclamation of Christ as *kurios* and *basileus* manifested its awareness of a realistic social and political operation of the Gospel. This challenge to the illegitimate powers of the age was rooted in the eschatology of the Gospel, our understanding of which, he regretted, had been "lost in a false, i.e., otherworldly, view of it."

I close these reminiscences of a bygone generation of workers in our field. Even such a fragmentary recital will have served its purpose if it reminds us not only of the way we have come but of the many aspects of our discipline and the various ways in which it relates to the wider issues of any period.

5

Albert Schweitzer and the New Testament

The greatness of Albert Schweitzer appears especially in the fact that he can only rightly be honored by action in the line of his own commitments. The impulse to honorifics is human and pardonable, but even merited eulogies are like flattery in delaying action. One can see Schweitzer as restless during ceremonies. We do not mean to associate him with an inhuman and humorless austerity, but rather to

Though this paper goes back in its writing to 1962 there is much in it which makes it appropriate to the present collection. As I have noted above, it was my encounter with Albert Schweitzer at Oxford in 1922 which first aroused my lifelong interest in early Christian eschatology and crystallized my turn toward New Testament studies professionally. As a student then of C.H. Dodd I was much excited by Schweitzer's *Quest of the Historical Jesus* and the issues which it raised. This scholar's attempt to do justice to Jesus' view of his mission and the future in terms of Jewish eschatology was, as I have also noted above, illuminated for me by my World War I experience of apocalyptic ordeal, utopian vision and foreshortened expectation. In exploring the psychology of this dramatizing outlook I was led to my wider interest in the interpretation of myth and of the imaginative aspects of biblical tradition, both of which it seemed to me had been overlooked in our historical criticism.

This discussion is likewise relevant to my accompanying article on Norman Perrin. In that paper also I mention the work of Erich Grässer who has since published an overdue assessment of Schweitzer's theological premises, *Albert Schweitzer als Theolog* (1979).

This study despite its date may have a compensating interest in that it reflects the controversial response to Schweitzer at the time when neo-orthodoxy and existentialism were widely influential.

This essay was written for *In Albert Schweitzer's Realms,* ed. A.A. Roback (Cambridge, Mass.: Sci-Art Publishers, 1962), copyright now held by the Albert Schweitzer Memorial Foundation, Inc., of Wallingford, Connecticut. I am indebted to its officers, including the honoree's daughter, Rhena Schweitzer Miller, and Harold E. Robles, for permission to republish it here.—A.N.W.

underline how far his gracious single-mindedness is from personal complacencies. We may, however, be sure that he will be indulgent to our various testimonies so far as in them his own concerns are reflected.

If we say that Schweitzer can best be honored by action in the line of his own commitments, we do not mean by practical humanitarian activity alone. His commitments have included intellectual labors in many fields, including religious history and especially the study of Christian origins. We can honor him by furthering clarification here, and we can honor him, too, not only by agreement but by disagreement, provided that we keep in mind the aphorism from St. Paul that meant so much to him: "We cannot do anything against the truth but only for the truth." That is, if we are right, the truth will prevail; if we are wrong, the truth will prevail. It is our business to pursue the truth as best we can. But we rejoice that truth will vindicate itself by us or against us.

It is regrettable that there is so considerable a divergence between the following of Albert Schweitzer and the dominant theological trend today, or if we can put it more widely, between liberal Christianity and neo-Protestantism. So far as concerns Schweitzer's thought and its influence, this divergence no doubt rests back on real differences in historical judgments about Jesus and the beginnings of the church. One object of this paper is to suggest some mitigation of these differences. This inevitably requires some criticism and correction of both sides, together with defense of the insights on both sides. But since the liberal side has less of a hearing in the actual theological situation, we shall give more attention to the claims it may rightly make, both with respect to historical reconstruction of the New Testament and to a modern understanding of Christianity.

In the religious and theological differences of today, especially with respect to those between liberal and conservative, or liberal and neo-orthodox, the best appeal against dogmatism on either side and the best appeal for truly ecumenical appreciation is that to humility. This is a virtue more often, but not always, found in the liberal. In any case, what should make all humble is not only the dimension of the human need to be met, but above all the inevitably very wide gamut of forms in which our religious tradition will communicate itself in the conditions of our culture. The differences of theological views are largely due to nontheological factors. Our so different messages represent on the whole the same original life impulse from Jesus of Nazareth in different dialects determined by different cultural and philosophical traditions. The life example of Albert Schweitzer on the one hand, or for that matter the example of the Friends today, or for that matter that of many nonconfessing "Christians," merely evidence the fortunate multiplicity of ways in which the impact of Christ's life makes itself felt in our world whose cultural pluralism ever surprises us. Orthodoxy or neo-orthodoxy, this denominationalism or that sectarianism, this school or that -ism should moderate their claims and their acerbity, remembering that their particular formulations are relative to particular backgrounds. The truth lies with all rather than with any one of them, or rather it lies behind and before all.

What liberalism should concede in the various forms of neo-orthodoxy today is their willingness to take on the immense intellectual task of wrestling with the whole history of Christian thought as well as with ancient and contemporary philosophies. Theology in this sense is the transmission and criticism of the family records of the Christian household. Religion has to do this just as an instructed patriotism has to carry out an analogous self-examination. An emancipated modernism, whether in religion or in patriotism, tends to shun this task, in part, as can be well understood, because such family annals and traditions often have a kind of ghetto character. Schweitzer himself has set an example of this kind of responsibility in his work both on the New Testament and on the philosophy of civilization. His contribution in either area, however, as he would be the first to admit, will only be finally defined in dialogue with the ongoing investigation by all concerned.

What the new theological movements should concede to the various forms of liberalism today is above all their right to formulate the religious traditions of the West in this or that special language meaningful to the groups concerned. Why should the continental Reformation have the dominant import for all Western Christianity that it naturally has for those bodies directly related to it, as it were, by blood and soil! There may and should be vigorous challenge and query, thrust and parry, between Protestants and Catholics, between

Lutherans and Calvinists, between orthodox and liberal; but all parties should take due account of the various climates of thought and habit and sensibility in terms of which any one of them speaks.

A lot of water has passed under the bridge since Schweitzer first published his views of Jesus and the Gospels. No informed scholarship since has been able to undercut the major contribution here, namely, that Jesus, an alien to our modern ideas and rooted in his own time and place, saw history and the world in terms of the late Jewish apocalyptic eschatology of his background, though he gave this outlook his own creative interpretation. Schweitzer's thought here made a new epoch in our understanding of Christian origins.

Moreover, by unflinchingly carrying through these insights, Schweitzer, though he would have seemed to make Jesus irrelevant to later history, actually made him more relevant. Just because Jesus' inherited world conceptions could be recognized in all their archaic and obsolete character, it was possible for Schweitzer to identify more clearly—in his own somewhat idealistic terminology and rationalist categories indeed—that in them and behind them which was permanently potent and relevant to human life, not in some ulterior world but in this world. The best illustration of this outcome is his own life. Walter Lowrie once wrote me that Schweitzer had characterized his work in Africa as, in his understanding, "eschatology in action." That is, it is an attempt to carry through in a modern situation that urgent and hopeful striving, that application of optimistic moral will for human well-being, which animated the career of Jesus. As Schweitzer himself says:

> Those who see the goal which we are trying to reach, who do not remain indifferent but ever and again are touched by fear and suffering for the future of the world, are in a position truly to understand what the historical Jesus has to say to us, however alien his own language may be to us.[1]

Now it is true that our current biblical scholarship and theology accept the eschatological outlook of the historical Jesus and recognize the problem of translating it and of demythologizing it. But it does not proceed so radically as Schweitzer, and perhaps therefore

---

1. Albert Schweitzer, *The Quest of the Historical Jesus: A Critical Study of Its Progress from Reimarus to Wrede,* 2d ed. (New York: Macmillan, 1968).

carries over into modern Christian world view and ethic an undue remnant of dualism and unexamined dogma. It is right as against Schweitzer or, say, against Harnack, in retaining more of the religious and theological context and sanction of the moral life, or at least of spelling this out more particularly in terms of tradition. But in the interests of faith it sacrifices ethics, as the church has so characteristically done ever since; as Schweitzer shows, Paul's vital balance of faith and eschatology (Kingdom of God concern) became disassociated.

Schweitzer associates our understanding of Jesus' deepest intention with our capacity for being "touched by fear and suffering for the future of the world." Rudolf Bultmann for his part would associate it with a similar selflessness identified with obedience to the claims of God, that claim involving also our love for men. Ernst Fuchs, again, would describe it as identifying ourselves with Christ in his great principle of losing life to save it, also in terms of love. What strikes us immediately is that the formulations of Bultmann and Fuchs are apparently conventionally biblical-theological and somewhat individualistic, while Schweitzer's is refreshingly humanitarian. Yet behind Schweitzer's view of the believer's relation to Jesus is a profound religious, indeed Christian, mysticism which is only *not* theologically formulated because Schweitzer is not characteristically interested in spelling out such matters. We might indeed reasonably ask him to say in more detail just how it is that Jesus' world-affirming will, how the love which motivated Jesus, transmitted itself through and beyond the cross to his followers. Schweitzer rightly posits this fact; biblical theology seeks to articulate this process of revelation and grace in the light of the records and thus inevitably finds itself involved in issues of "theology" which Schweitzer leaves as a mystery. We may invoke here as illustrative Schweitzer's famous words: "As one unknown and nameless he comes to us . . ." and again: "til they come to know as an inexpressible secret who he is." Thus Schweitzer speaking as a liberal nevertheless appeals to mystery. On the other hand some of the contemporary biblical theologians, while sounding more or less dogmatic, can nevertheless appeal to the use of modern man's thought; for example, Bultmann, with whose view is associated a highly modern and even secular philosophical rationale, associated with Heidegger, one so modern that it has scandalized the orthodox on all sides. Similarly with Fuchs, who when seen in his own school is surprisingly radical: criticism of Barth, questioning of Bultmann, rejection of orthodox supernaturalism.

Schweitzer's principle of carrying any insight or commitment through to its ultimate consequences—"My task is to carry an idea through to its very end"—has the merit of opening up every possible bearing and ramification of a new factor. This procedure forces radical reconsideration all along the line and breaks up the most stubborn crust of stereotyped views, ideologies, or hackneyed patterns. It is the way of a kind of salutary violence. So an equinoctial storm sweeps away dead limbs and branches and prepares the way for spring. It carries the blessing of needed one-sided emphasis and hyperbole.

But it is just at this point that we can see why certain elements of Schweitzer's work on the New Testament have called for reassessment without, we insist, compromising the main contributions which we have noted. We do not propose here to go into the intricacies of New Testament criticism. In any case, the movement of scientific study of the Gospels away from his position on various important points is familiar.[2] It is not surprising in the light of the advance of all scientific frontiers in the course of the decades. The attempt of the so-called Bern School to repristinate Schweitzer's handling of the text of the Gospels at certain main points has not commended itself.[3] We can however single out one very live issue today rising out of

2. We may list briefly: the widely questioned interpretation of Matthew 10, and especially of Matt. 10:23, so important to his whole scheme; the interpretation of the mystery of the Kingdom of God in terms of its being "forced" and hastened by the action of Jesus and his disciples and later by Jesus' own deliberately sought death; the assignment to the outlook of Jesus of a fixed apocalyptic program taken over from Daniel, the Book of Enoch, and from other Jewish writings—a program to be lived through by himself and his followers; the absence of what has come to be better understood as form-critical criteria in the use of the Gospels; the definition of Jesus' ethic as "interim ethic" (though of course recognizing its eschatological conditioning in other ways).

3. Note the reactions of W. Michaelis, *Zur Engelchristologie im Urchristentum,* 1942; *Der Herr verzieht nicht die Verheissung,* 1942; Oscar Cullmann, *Le Retour du Christ,* 1945; "Das wahre durch die ausgebliebene Parusie gestellte neut. Problem," *Theologische Zeitschrift,* 1947, pp. 177ff; 422ff; 428ff; "Parusieverzögerung und Urchristentum," *Theologische Literaturzeitung,* 83,1 (Jan. 1958): 1–12; W.G. Kümmel, *Promise and Fulfillment,* 1957; Hermann Schuster, "Die konsequente Eschatologie in der Interpretation des Neuen Testaments," *Zeitschrift für neutestamentliche Wissenschaft,* 1956, pp. 1–25; G. Bornkamm, "Die Verzögerung der Parusie," in *In Memoriam E. Lohmeyer,* ed. W. Schmauch (Stuttgart, 1951), pp. 116–26.

Schweitzer's eschatological views, which the Swiss scholar Martin Werner has quickened. Here too we see how Schweitzer's drive toward the "thoroughgoing" or the "all or nothing" has both uncovered unsuspected depth and at the same time called forth persuasive correction. The point to make here again is that we are ultimately indebted to Schweitzer for the disclosure and clarification of sleeping issues precisely where final conclusions argue against his own original thrust.[4] We have reference to the discussion of the effects in the early church of the "delay of the Parousia," the shock to the church of the fact that Christ did not return as expected. Schweitzer and his followers have found here the key to the doctrines, especially after Paul. As Schweitzer writes:

> From the second generation onward the arrival of the Kingdom becomes "one far off divine event," and in later days it is infinitely far away. This change of necessity affects the nature of the expectation. Originally it held a dominant position at the very center of the faith; now it falls into the background. Instead of being the very essence of belief, it is now just one article among others.[5]

Schweitzer then goes on to show the results of this change: a sense of hopelessness about the now continuing world, the cutting of the nerve of meliorative activity, preoccupation of the individual with his own salvation, faith directed now rather to the resurrection to come and to forgiveness of sins than to realization of the present resurrection of the believer and faith and action oriented to the imminent and total Kingdom of God.

To put all this in more simple terms, Schweitzer sees the development and shaping of Christian belief and the attendant weaknesses, if not degeneration, of the later church—with various partially redeeming features and periods—as due in large part[6] to unsuccessful

---

4. Thus Schweitzer's identification of Jesus' ethic as "interim ethic" together with his view of the eschatological view of Jesus obliged scholarship to recognize fully the eschatological conditioning of Jesus' imperatives, and incidentally led to more satisfying views of their variety and their bearing than is suggested by that designation.

5. Cited from Schweitzer's paper, "The Conception of the Kingdom of God in the Transformation of Eschatology," in *The Theology of Albert Schweitzer for Christian Inquirers* by E.N. Mozley (London: Black, 1950), 82.

6. Schweitzer is more cautious here than some of his followers. He lists other factors along with that of disappointment over the Parousia, namely, "the struggle for unity, the conflict with second century Gnosticism, and accommodation to Greek metaphysic," ibid., 80–81.

attempts to come to terms with the unfulfilled promise of Jesus' return, especially with the surrender of the eschatological idea of the Kingdom of God.

It is true that Martin Werner has developed the theme that the nonfulfillment of the promise of the Parousia was the decisive factor in the development of Christian dogma. It is also true that scholars have utilized these insights in dealing with this or that particular New Testament writing: for example, Hans Conzelmann with reference to Luke-Acts[7] or Erich Grässer with respect to many of the New Testament writings.[8] But the weight of authority today tends toward the view that the fading of the end-expectation did not constitute a crisis for the main body of the church. The life of the movement rested on deeper sources than this particular mythical time-conception. It is a mistake to assign either to Jesus or to the early church such a hard and fast apocalyptic schema that disappointments with the schedule would have been catastrophic. The first believers were not like some modern adventists in a prosaic-minded calculation of the times. To think so is to misunderstand the mythical mentality of the early church. Evidently there was questioning with regard to the calendar of God's plan in some quarters even in the first century and even in the time of Paul. And there were great changes looking toward formalization of belief, rite and time-conceptions. But these changes took place out of a positive drive to self-expression in new circumstances rather than out of a defensive remedy for delayed hopes.

Nevertheless, we must credit Schweitzer with having brought to the fore the danger of a false dualism and false spirituality consequent upon the theological developments after Paul. Paul had a realistic idea of world transformation here and now, all linked up with the believer's own redemption. Later these two were divorced, and the faith lost much of its real impact on the historical process even in so temporal a regime as that of Constantine. Schweitzer believes, however, that since the eighteenth century in association with Enlightenment attitudes Protestantism is

> moving in the direction of a philosophy of world acceptance . . . belief
> in the kingdom of God now takes a new lease on life. It no longer

---

7. Cf. H. Conzelmann, "Gegenwart und Zukunft in der syn. Tradition," *Zeitschrift für Theologie und Kirche* 54 (1957): 227–96.

8. Erich Grässer, *Das Problem der Parusieverzögerung in den syn. Evangelien und in der Apostelgeschichte,* 1957.

looks for its coming, self-determined, as an eschatological cosmic event, but regards it as something ethical and spiritual, not bound up with the last things, but to be realized with the cooperation of men.[9]

Schweitzer notes that this view of the coming Kingdom is not that of Jesus and Paul. Yet "if it is *historically* wrong, it is *religiously* right."

In spite of many fundamental differences from the past, modern Protestant Christianity remains true to the gospel since it is still a religion of the living faith in the kingdom of God.[10]

Schweitzer is here affirming those modern aspects of a liberal Christianity which recent neo-Protestantism and neo-orthodoxy have decried. We may note, however, that Schweitzer insists on the religious and indeed the New Testament roots of this Christian attitude and would be as opposed as any exponent of "biblical realism" to Christian secularism or to a sell-out of the faith to pagan totalitarianism or to any kind of cultural pagan confusion. We may also note that Schweitzer is at one with Bultmann and with many of the most vital continental theologians today in excluding a view of revelation dependent upon supernaturally miraculous events and evidences *(Heilstatsachen)*.

The fact is that the main currents of traditional theology today have been shocked into new vitality by the political and cultural situation of our time and have gone a long way toward emancipation from conventional dogma and rigidity. The earlier liberalization incident to the history of biblical criticism has facilitated this quickening, as indeed it underlay also the work of Schweitzer himself. What remains is for our contemporary "realistic theology" not indeed to give over its own line of development, but to recognize its particularity, its partiality, to recognize that it represents only one formulation among many possible and that various forms of liberal theology have equivalent claims to essential insights.

What we are pleading for is, therefore, recognition of the wide spectrum of vital contemporary expressions of Christianity. Positively, this suggests the many-sided options with reference to the Christian heritage offered to modern man: from Barth, say, to Christian humanism or, indeed, from the new evangelical orthodoxy on the

9. "The Conception of the Kingdom of God in the Transformation of Eschatology," 100–101.

10. Ibid., 102.

right to the Quakers, Unitarians and Universalists on the left. Schweitzer's type is one effective outreach in circles where other options are not persuasive. Negatively, this suggests that—so far as the heritage of the Reformation is concerned—the recently renewed neo-Protestantism, largely Lutheran in its formulation and increasingly identified with existentialism, is thrown on the defensive in its claim to speak for Western faith and indeed in its claim to represent a normative view of the New Testament gospel. At the heart of Schweitzer's New Testament interpretation we find a view of Paul which subordinates the doctrine of justification by faith alone to the Pauline theme of eschatological mysticism. This emphasis relates Schweitzer's conception of Paul to that of Greek Orthodoxy and represents a parting of the ways in the New Testament itself from the theology and biblical theology so widely influential today. Schweitzer holds that the juridical formulations of the Epistle to the Romans had a particular occasion and do not lead us to the center of Paul's view of the Christian life.

We may add that just as the theme of the Epistle to the Romans was especially conditioned by the particular problem of the Jewish law, so the Reformation emphasis on justification by faith alone was conditioned by the special problem of Catholic legal and juridical patterns, just as contemporary neo-orthodoxy is conditioned by the special problem of modern guilt and modern cultural authority and false authority—reaching its intolerable form in totalitarianism. On all these occasions the theme of freedom versus bondage is thrust to the fore, and justification by faith alone is a relevant evangelical emphasis. The Christian battle with the times on these occasions and in these terms was and is enormously fruitful, but the part should not be taken for the whole. It is indispensable that other emphases in the recovery of Christianity today should supplement this current emphasis, and here Schweitzer and his followers have much to say. There are other modern emphases, including the heritage of the left wing of the Reformation, which similarly enrich the available options of Christian influence and renewal today, emphases which may be called neoliberal or may even take the form of a nonconfessional or "latent" Christianity which may be highly influential and salutary in Western life.

It is worth noting here that biblical exegesis and theology today in those circles which have been most closely identified with neo-orthodoxy are evidencing rifts and questionings. Such questions are asked as: How much is left of the New Testament canon if justification by faith alone is taken as the only norm? What about Luke-Acts? What about the Gospel of Matthew? Or: How can one render full justice to the Old Testament if the Pauline juridical atonement themes are given such prominence? Or: How can a modern Christian ethic be formulated in this context? Lutheran views of the gospel have always had their heel of Achilles here in this matter of ethics, and neo-Protestant views of Paul's ethic only highlight this disability which in our present world situation takes on a formidable significance. Schweitzer's view of Paul as well as of the New Testament as a whole makes a welcome place, if not for a Christian moral table of duties today, at least for an undisparaged affirmation of Christian moral attack on injustice and inhumanity.

A second great contribution of Schweitzer to our contemporary religious situation is the following. If—with, no doubt, question-begging implications—we identify Schweitzer with Christian liberalism or neoliberalism, we note nevertheless that there is that in his "openness" which arrests liberalism on the slope toward religious humanism and eclecticism. Modernity has been so impressed by the ideal of impartiality and dispassionateness proper to method in much scientific operation, and has had such stumbling blocks and rigidities thrown in its way by narrow Christian orthodoxy, that many understandably move all the way over from a specific religious allegiance to what they think of as a wholly emancipated appreciation of all religions alike, if not indifference to all. They thus may confuse the necessary objectivity in limited scientific areas with uncommitted and neutral attitudes in significant life issues.

The individual who sees himself as a free spirit and one divested of parochial dogmatism and who acclaims Schweitzer as a Daniel come to judgment or who would even "appropriate" him meets with some surprises. We may note first the exalted place assigned by Schweitzer to Paul and to Paul's Christ-mysticism rather than God-mysticism. Schweitzer, indeed, disparages the juristic-rabbinic elements in Paul, but he refuses to accept the clichés that the Christian cult was significantly influenced by Mithraism or any of the Hellenistic mystery religions, or resembles them. Again, Schweitzer cannot be taken as a proponent of the theme that all of the high religions say essentially the same thing, or that the great Eastern religions in their original inspiration testify to reverence for life in the sense that Schweitzer understands it, as associated with love and with the moral will directed to the fulfillment of life in this world. Moreover, Schweitzer has a genuine doctrine of revelation in the sense that no one can grasp or be grasped by an operative reverence for life except in terms of an awakening at the roots of his or her being, where love is mystically kindled and empowered.

There is no finally effective check in the current forms of orthodoxy or neo-orthodoxy to the widespread movement today toward religious relativism, a movement which often is confused with a noble and universal magnanimity and tolerance. Schweitzer's type of Christian life and thought offers a place in the *Christian* tradition for the person attracted by humanism, skepticism, positivism. And he does this not only by the example of his disinterested life devotion and his catholic sympathies, both religious and cultural, but also by an intellectual defense of Christianity grounded in historical research and in historical judgment. Schweitzer as a Christian apologist can appeal to many as one who offers sound credentials as a rationalist—a rationalist who carries his rationalism through instead of stopping halfway. For human reason must come to terms with many realities in man and in history which rationalism as usually defined has never faced.

6

Norman Perrin, Historical Knowledge and Faith

Erich Grässer is particularly well known for his earlier study of the problem of the delay of the Parousia.[1] In 1979 he published *Albert Schweitzer als Theologe*,[2] a wide-ranging examination of the central problem as it arises in the work of this controversial pioneer.

Norman Perrin's American colleagues were particularly grateful to Grässer for his share in the memorial tribute in *The Journal of Religion*. It was highly appropriate and gratifying that one of the contributions should have come from a German scholar who had been personally acquainted with the circles and teachers which had influenced Norman both in his study years and in his later work.

Grässer notes that both the difficulty of Perrin's long pilgrimage and the spur to it can be traced to the fact that he early came under the influence of his *Doktorvater* Joachim Jeremias (after studying in England with T.W. Manson) but also that of Rudolf Bultmann. The

Norman Perrin died in November, 1976. In 1984 a memorial issue of *The Journal of Religion* in his honor was published (vol. 64, no. 4). Among the tributes to him in this issue was an especially searching article by his friend Erich Grässer of the University of Bonn, entitled "Norman Perrin's Contribution to the Question of the Historical Jesus" (pp. 484–500). The considerations raised in this paper about the relation of history to faith, not only in Perrin's work but in our modern period generally, lead me to the following reflections on this continuing problem.—A.N.W.

This chapter originally appeared in *The Harvard Theological Review* 82 (1989), copyright 1989 by the President and Fellows of Harvard College. Reprinted by permission.

1. *Das Problem der Parusieverzögerung* (Berlin, 1957, 1977).
2. (Tübingen: J.C.B. Mohr [Paul Siebeck]).

attempt to validate these two differing standpoints led him to explore new ground with respect to the problem of the historical Jesus.

In his article Grässer pays respect to the searching and cogent procedure of Perrin as he sought to establish the contribution of criticism to our understanding of the kerygmatic testimony of the early tradition and to the Christian faith in all times. Notable here is Perrin's threefold distinction with respect to our "knowledge" of Jesus Christ: (1) "historical" knowledge, that is, factual, objective, documentable, all from an uninvolved standpoint; (2) "historic" (*geschichtliche* as vs. *historische*) knowledge which "examines the past in the light of its significance for the present" and therefore "existentially." This overlaps the first, but any neutral data are absorbed in the total apprehension and are indistinguishable in the existential encounter; (3) "faith knowledge" whose qualitative difference from either rests on the kerygmatic recognition of Jesus as Lord and Christ shared with the community.

Perrin, like Bultmann, wished to keep these three kinds of knowledge apart (which the "new hermeneutic" fails to do). But then he moves *beyond* Bultmann by attempting to show how historical reflection and analysis can have *theological* relevance. Findings with regard to the *historical* Jesus, his deeds and words, can have a "maieutic, corrective and paradigmatic significance for faith," whose main source, however, remains the Easter kerygma (Grässer, p. 496).

Grässer sees a gain in Perrin's analysis and cites appreciation of it by Käsemann, Ebeling and others. He himself goes on to ask for more attention to the person of Jesus since the supposed correspondence of the historical Jesus and the Christ of faith requires clear identification at this point. Is not the Easter proclamation which "opens up a radically new eschatological dimension" (p. 498) of so different an order from what may be learned from the sifting of pre-Easter tradition that the former may be clouded by the latter? "Plainly, the relation that exists between the historical and the theological viewpoints surfaces here as a fundamental problem that requires further clarification" (p. 498).

It is to be recalled here that Perrin had built a persuasive argument for relevance of the historical founder to the Christology of the evangelists and the early community by noting the way in which sayings of the Lord, whether pre- or post-Easter, were cited as equally authoritative. Perrin also found similar continuity between situations and challenges portrayed in the course of the historical ministry and those which the New Testament authors addressed. Thus in various ways the later believers oriented to the risen Christ and the new age testify to the identity for them of Jesus of Nazareth and the risen Lord.

But it is this equation which, Grässer urges, requires further historical-critical clarification. After all, the kerygmatic formulations of the early church in all their plurality may not necessarily have been reliably linked with the founder and with God's work in "the days of his flesh." "Of course," writes Grässer, "the early Christian kerygma must not be measured exclusively against the history of Jesus. What is required is a hermeneutic of continuous circularity from the Jesus of history to the kerygmatic Christ and back again" (p. 499).

Grässer has here contributed both a discerning appreciation of Norman Perrin's labors in this crucial area and pointed to further tasks. If he suggests that the question of the historical Jesus will remain an *aporia*, yet our modern approach to it, in its theological bearings, is presented with notable clarity. But the whole discussion suggests some wider considerations relative to Perrin's work and the issues it raises.

One latent issue that arises with respect to Norman Perrin's work is that of the wider presuppositions on which it is based. It is a question of the historical context, the "school-context," the hermeneutical tradition and setting in which a scholar works. In this respect one can urge that Perrin's approach and tools and categories were "situated." No doubt all such historical reconstructions are "situated," but it is illuminating to take account of such particular controls on our work and our strategies. It is recognized, for example, that Norman Perrin himself was initiated into and found himself divided between two quite different orientations to historical work, those of T.W. Manson and Jeremias on the one hand and Bultmann on the other. The difference, apart from local praxis and immediate agenda, is ontological, a question of world and world-historical apperception. No one and no scholar can ever bridge or transcend such an a priori without quandaries and without remainders.

Grässer rightly notes that in his later writing Perrin moved toward the Bultmann stance. From Luther to Bultmann to Perrin we recognize the outlook in which the "Word" or kerygma is the determining focus of faith. Here "history" as the lived involvement of the People of God from the origins on, also in the New Testament, is taken up into faith and witness. Any approach to it as objective and neutral record is inappropriate as well as inadequate. This is already evident in the fact that the early believers knew nothing of our kind of historical interest and method and wrote without this kind of concern.

But cannot one say that Bultmann's presupposition here, granted its fruitfulness and influence, was very particularly "situated," and that even Perrin's modified version of it can be moved into a different and wider frame? This would be one in which "history" can be more fully honored, yet without a return to the categories of Jeremias and the older liberal procedures.

In the context in which Perrin and other post-Bultmannians worked, the gap between historical method with its findings and either the primitive kerygma or modern faith appears to have been peculiarly constitutive of theological labors. While this gulf could be justified by appeal to the categories of revelation and the Word, yet it took on a particular sanction in the modern situation with which we are concerned. We have to do with a sharp dichotomy between history and faith which was "situated" on the one hand, no doubt, by the church-struggle of the period but also more generally by current epistemological assumptions.

In this setting one can find other influential figures besides Bultmann for whom historical research was either deprecated or seen as only ambiguously related to kerygma and revelation. Besides Karl Barth the position of Albert Schweitzer is particularly interesting. Grässer in the study of Schweitzer mentioned above shows that while this author of the famous *Quest* insisted on the historicity of Jesus as an indispensable given, yet especially in his later correspondence he registered his disparagement of all such tools of Gospel study as form criticism and redaction criticism. His Jesus was a mystery and a power far above the reach of such investigations. In the field of theology Paul Tillich is an example of the influence of such hermeneutical wrestlings in the period. In his case also significant affirmation about the Christ could only be reached by one or other kind of leap beyond "historicism."

It would appear that even in his later work Norman Perrin labored under the restraints of a prior and systematic dichotomy between historical knowledge and faith-apprehension. This situation is still with us as many ask how we can ground the great affirmations of the gospel on the kind of uncertain, fragmentary, naive and often contradictory evidence provided for us in our first-century sources. The actualities of those episodes and agencies are seen as irretrievable by historical investigation. An analogy is found in what seems the irrelevance of the analysis of musicologists to our enjoyment of a Beethoven symphony.

Yet the integral continuity of the church's proclamation with the foregoing empirical transactions should be a basic premise. Any slighting of the importance of our evidences for the initial phases of this process undermines the continuity, and the resulting formulations, reached by one or other "leap" over the hidden annals, will be suspect.

While Rudolf Bultmann did more than anyone to investigate the baffling records, yet the presuppositions of his version of the kerygmatic faith disallowed the significance and even the appropriateness of the critical findings. In his case a neo-Kantian existentialist focus on the basic human category of the *conatus*, the will, choice, decision, obedience, took priority over the faculties of knowing and affect (feeling and imagination). In this anthropology, therefore, both historical knowledge and mythological representation could not be seen as aspects of a holistic human apprehension and response. The result was to that extent a dehistoricized kerygma which, nevertheless, represented a powerful if situated translation of the gospel.

Albert Schweitzer, as his culture-historical writings show, still reflected a liberal Enlightenment ontology, but his demand for what he called an "elementary thinking" led to a critique of rationalism and therefore of historical criticism as generally practiced. His "historical Jesus" therefore had a mystical character, one whose power could animate any subsequent world view apart from any wrestling with the ancient records. His own exercise in this area in *Das Abendmahl* and the *Quest* only pointed to the *aporia* of the outcome of the ministry of Jesus and its discontinuity with any sequel.

In remembering also the presuppositions behind the work of Karl Barth, the question today is whether a new frame or paradigm can be identified by which this dichotomy between history and faith can be overcome and which would enable us to deal with the records in the Gospels and in early Christianity more productively in relation to the church's confessions. This presumably would go beyond the assumptions of those today pursuing the sociological study of early Christianity or of other new approaches to the historical Jesus, most of whom are content to illuminate the data in their ancient context as prolegomena to any eventual faith-formulations. In dealing with "The Jesus of History and the Christ of Faith" we look for an approach in which the continuity can be identified without either derogating the historical-critical operations or diminishing the significance of the Resurrection and the eschatological hope.

I believe that the whole question can be placed in a new light if we can adopt a view of the past and of the flow of historical tradition more adequate to the richness and complexity of temporal experience. Our modern categories of historiography with their quest for rationality and objectivity have understandably lifted out causal and relational sequences from the total web of transactions reported in the sources. But this means that a one-dimensional or skeletal account is given of a multidimensional reality. Even when historians seek to enrich or deepen their reporting by empathy and interpretation the restraints of method condemn them to an abstracted purview.

A striking corollary of this situation is afforded by the fact that as regards the history of the church and its origins we make so much of the beginnings of historical method and criticism in the eighteenth century. This furthers the idea of two epochs in the latter of which alone any proper concern with historical reality was felt. This also encourages a narrowed view of history confined to those aspects of it most immediately controlled and exhibited by the appropriate strategies of the science in question. But there are many happenings both ancient and modern which would elude this kind of scrutiny and which may have great importance, yet which are still open to other kinds of appropriate assessment.

Although their horizons and perspectives on time were not ours we should recognize that the earliest witnesses to the Gospel events and the authors of our Gospels and other writings had a crucial concern with what we call history and a life or death stake in the reality of the transactions, in our terms "psychological" and "social," which they reported. If their "world" had what seem to us fictional and surreal features their scenarios and modes of narration were nevertheless dictated by their experience and were all the more faithful to their heightened theater of observation.

As regards their concern for responsible reporting our current interest in "story" should not lead us to minimize the prior claims of historical truth as they understood it. Without citing here such recurrent asseverations of veracity as we find in Paul and in Luke-Acts or the tone and tenor of the Gospels generally with their emphasis on the fatefulness of the record, we may take as representative the opening of John's first Epistle: "That . . . which we have heard, which we have seen with our eyes, which we have looked upon, and our hands have handled . . . declare we unto you. . . ."

As regards the heightened theater of their reporting, which included what for us were nonempirical agencies and events, we should recognize that different ages have differing sensibilities and are at home in differing intellectual-imaginative worlds. While empirical experience may for them have been associated with what we would call mythological agencies and horizons, yet it is through such categories that they apprehend and report experience, an experience and a reality not discontinuous with ours. In some societies, in situations in which the gamut of experience is heightened, depths and heights of the human lot may come into view, and the records or narrations of such versions of our world should be fully honored by the historian.

The mentality of the early Christian movement is a case in point. Our Christian historiography should press behind its own modern canons and find ways to accommodate the primitive testimonies in a richer and more total portrayal. What is particularly to the point here in these reflections is that the systematic dichotomy between historical knowledge and faith could be overcome, conditioned as it has been by a reductionist approach to history.

What stands in the way of such a revision of method is our long-standing "historical conscience" and its circumscribed view of evidence as factual, objective, neutral. The concern for truth indeed remains paramount, and investigation at whatever level will always be germane, but illumination of such a heightened *sensorium* as that behind the gospel beginnings and of its documents calls for its own kind of appropriate tests.

Our indebtedness to the pioneers of biblical criticism cannot be exaggerated, and we can agree with Albert Schweitzer in his well-known concluding tribute to the inestimable "value of what German research upon the life of Jesus has accomplished" as "a uniquely great expression of sincerity." But Christendom had always had its memory, its continuity with its origins and its own kind of ever-renewed reappropriation of that heritage from the beginning, a reappropriation guided by its own kind of precritical discriminations. The phase of modern historical criticism can best be seen, therefore, as a *sophistication* of the more general wrestling of the church with its past, a phase whose findings still remain to be illuminated by the more total assessment. One point at which our critical canons can be thus deepened and "history" more adequately evoked is the recognition of what I am here concerned with, the surrealist and preternatural mentality reflected in our texts, a world which eludes our usual charting. It is not enough to point here to the ways in which modern criticism and interpretation have dealt with myth, miracle, imagery and mysticism. It is a question not of topic and detail but of the lens through which all happening is viewed.

An analogy of this task can be found in T.S. Eliot's essay on Dante.[3] Dealing with the visionary mentality of that epoch and of the Provençal poets and other poets cherished by Dante, Eliot is led to reflect on "the world of the high dream" which he then associates with *The Divine Comedy*, the *Vita Nuova*, and the Book of Revelation (p. 223). It was an age in which men still saw visions: ". . . we have nothing but dreams" (p. 204). For us, Eliot writes, "it is as hard as a rebirth to pass through the looking glass into a world which is just as reasonable as our own. When we have done that, we begin to wonder whether the world of Dante is not both larger and more solid than our own" (p. 236).

We should not underestimate the difference between the sensibility of the early Christians and our own. But neither should we exaggerate it.

---

3. *Selected Essays*, 1917–32 (New York: Harcourt, Brace, & Co., 1932).

One can say that they lived as under a spell, in a mental and imaginative climate, whose "strong persuasion," featured by ancient myth and eschatological vision, colored their empirical experience. Such archives of this unique world-apprehension as those we have in our Gospels convey to us their reading of the momentous historical drama in question in the light of their intensified apperception. In the successive phases of the tradition we can, no doubt, recognize shifts toward realism as the mystique evolved. But the narration of Jesus' ministry still took on a preternatural character answering to the higher octaves and registers of their perception. Thus many rightly assign the Gospel of Mark to the genre-form of apocalypse rather than to that of *vita*.

Such considerations should lead us to keep open the kinds of tests and calibrations we employ in seeking "history" in such texts. In them what we call "fact" or actuality is not only indissociable from the visionary context but is determined and qualified by it. Realism and surrealism are merged. It may be objected that here or there references are made to actual historical data of the period such as "in the days of Herod the King" or identification of such figures as Caiaphas and Pilate. But while such "secular" history is sometimes evoked as notably by the author of Luke-Acts its purport is taken up into the prior and larger story.

In this kind of narrative not only is fact subsumed in the prophetic and visionary perspective but "history" in its aspects of sequence and plot is seen and experienced in the light of a higher ordering and of prototypical dramas. Just as spatial features such as desert and city, Egypt and Holy Land, Galilee and Jerusalem, may be mapped by what has been called "theological geography," so events in time, whether genealogies or periodizations ("three days," "forty days") or hostile powers or fateful episodes are shaped and charged by an all-encompassing *Heilsgeschichte*. Thus historical sequence, agency and outcome are portrayed through the lens of this particular "high dream." If we seek to impose our dichotomy of history/faith (and both terms of the distinction reflect our own categories) we should be aware that we are subverting the holism of the ancient portrayal. The extremes of such modern distortion date back to a time when all that could not be elicited as factual history in the Gospels was simply identified as superstition.

If the early traditions emerged from this kind of heightened sensibility or mythical mentality, we should also recognize the difficulty of those who would deal with the sociology of their background. All such features of a society as hierarchy, family, livelihood, wealth and poverty, slavery, demography, all these take on a radically different significance in different cultural settings with their differing metaphysical assumptions. This is why sociological analysis should be associated with rhetorical criticism since language and rhetoric reflect the social vision and mythology of a community. An illuminating exhibit of this double approach is afforded by Norman Petersen's study of Paul's Epistle to Philemon.[4]

I return to T.S. Eliot's discussion of Dante as an illustration of the issues in such texts. In the *Vita Nuova* first, and later in the *The Divine Comedy*, Dante narrates in highly symbolic ways at home in the sensibility of the age his first encounter with Beatrice and its meaning and sequel. What we call the facts of the meeting and its psychological and affective consequences are parts of the poet's real autobiography which historians seek to tease out from the imaginative nimbus in which it is clothed. But surely the way in which Dante evokes it is the way in which it really happened for him. As with any attempt to write a biography of Dante so it is with our procedures in recovering the historical Jesus and the beginnings of the church. Those versions will be most faithful to the Event and the events which, suspending our later categories, take full advantage of the horizon and modes and particulars of the original historical scenarios as they were experienced and reported by the early witnesses. This was for them "history" as they knew and lived it, with aspects of the heights and depths of empirical existence interwoven in the detail, all of which we should seek to carry over into our retelling.

In his later writing Norman Perrin was exploring a more adequate interpretive method. His options were still understandably influenced by the approach of Bultmann. But as I have noted this existentialist transcription of the Gospel scanted essential dimensions of the primitive proclamation. Thus the polarity of history and faith, with this particular and "situated" legacy, has still continued to character-

---

4. *Rediscovering Paul: Philemon and the Sociology of Paul's Narrative World* (Philadelphia: Fortress Press, 1985).

ize the hermeneutical task. Grässer concludes his discussion as follows: "Perrin's contribution to the problem of the historical Jesus is commendable in so far as it undertakes to build a bridge between extreme fronts. That the *aporia* of the historical Jesus as an issue of theological hermeneutics is not therewith resolved . . . may have been most obvious to, of all people, Perrin himself" (p. 500).

In my own reflections here I have sought to go behind our usual procedures and to suggest a horizon in which our quest may be more rewardingly pursued. We should seek to identify ourselves more willingly with the perspective of the ancient witnesses and with the surreal categories and idioms of their world-reading. Should we not recognize that we have to do here not just with mythology and prodigy but with an *episteme* radically different from our own with its own scale and gamut, and whose very energy or *zelos* challenges our codes? Before we intrude our own screen of appraisal upon its texts should we not, also as historians, expose ourselves fully to what may seem their arcane communication?

I recur to the original question as to how we can elicit what we mean by "history" from the kind of texts left us by the early witnesses. Is there a way by which we can readapt our lens or optics so that our transcription of the sources may be both more responsive to their full import while still satisfying our demand for an intelligible but nonreductive modern version?

As an analogy for this task one may return to Eliot's discussion of Dante's *Vita Nuova*. The actual empirical story of the poet's encounters with Beatrice is indeed *there* though sublimated and hidden in the particular nimbus of the language and symbol of the age.

It would be misleading to suppose that our task with the early texts is just another exercise in converting poetry into prose. Aside from the fact that this exercise can never be done, the imaginative discourse of Scripture has features even in its poetic strains which already distinguish it from poetry as commonly viewed. Prominent in it are such features of prose as predication, parenesis, argument: the discursive and the normative are fused with the plastic and the visionary. Northrop Frye, in his *The Great Code*, has written pointedly on this, observing that the Bible is indeed literature but something more. It is *kerygma*. We may add that the early kerygma and the Gospels do not only tell a story or stories but a world-story, and one shot through with intelligence *(intellectus)* as well as with vision. This "high dream" is structured, and with its episodes, epiphanies and oracles is oriented toward a denouement.

Any contemporary transcription of such alien revelatory discourse should seek to mediate both its surrealism and its particularity. As compared with other cultural mythologies it has a distinctive orientation, teleology and intentionality.

Our appropriation of the pristine witness in both aspects already has its antecedents, as I have noted, in the history of the church. During the long precritical epochs the societies of the faithful have had their own deep continuity with the origins and their own criteria for perpetuating it in teaching, liturgies and praxis.

Our later period as it has sought to identify an empirical history in the traditions has, indeed, been able to illuminate *those aspects which its focus and method could control.* But this has left a range of testimony unaccounted for, and a gap between the empirical and the visionary. At one level this disjuncture reflects the well-known "split of sensibility" associated with the Enlightenment. But given the theological import of the tradition it has meant a fateful dislocation between history and faith and between the historical Jesus and the Christ of faith.

This brings us back to Norman Perrin's problem with which we began. I have sought, however, to put it in a larger context. The total legacy, with regard to which we distinguish "history" and "faith," has had its integral continuity in the memory of the Christian people, for whom the original transactions have been both contemporary and remembered. The distinction between history and faith—both referring to the common story and witness—stems not from the legacy itself but from our modern perspective and the method associated with it. But this optic or *instrumentum*, with its categories of the empirical and controllable, has its limitations. History in the larger sense has its imponderables and its higher and more subtle registers of meaning which should enter into the account.

It is at this point that hermeneutic in our situation has its opportunity already anticipated by Perrin and others. In mediating between the world of the texts and our modern categories of inquiry the two different optics can illuminate each other.

Our modern canons of criticism, associated with an age of objec-
tivism and positivism, have already been undermined in our time and
are more open to a dynamic reality without forfeiting our commitment to the empirical, to lucidity and to discrimination. We can be
instructed by dimensions of experience in the past which we have
disallowed as oneiric, inchoate or obscurantist. But these essential
aspects of the tradition can be brought within our agenda and our
fuller portrayal of the history.

The procedures for this more adequate transcription of a dynamic
multifaceted world-story are already being opened up by probings
associated with related sociocultural studies as well as by literary and
rhetorical criticism. Such strategies should not be narrowly conceived
since the field of inquiry goes beyond particular communities or texts
to what has been called "the archaeology of the imagination." The
category of "imagination" (as of "social imagination") is crucial here.
But this term has so many associations, aesthetic, oneiric, romantic,
that it is hardly negotiable in the kind of discourse where we most
need it. But this only underlines the front at which hermeneutic is
engaged with diverse sensibilities, epistemes and their structures.

What is in view here, then, granted this richer repossession of the
primitive traditions, is a more adequate rehearsal in our own terms, *a
more appropriate historiography.* Thanks to our deeper penetration
of the sources we should be able to provide a truer account of the
historical Jesus and of Christian origins, if only in the sense that it
would be multidimensional. Such a contemporary account of the
foundational transactions will recognize the claims of the empirical
and the evidential. Our findings by way of historical criticism would
still be honored but taken up into the wider purview. Here such
categories as "empirical" and "evidential" would now relate to the
fuller spectrum of reality calling for appraisal.

Any such new version of the Jesus-story and the Christ-story
achieved by passing through the looking glass into that dynamic world
(which was, indeed, one of world-end and world-renewal) should
flesh out our empirical and documentable histories so that the
stubborn gap between history and faith will no longer require that
irrational "leap" so familiar in our period.

PART THREE

GENRES, RHETORICS AND MEANING

7

Wilder on Crossan
on Wilder

That the Society of Biblical Literature should have included me among
those to be assessed in its series I took as a recognition of the importance of those particular interpretive interests and soundings which
have long engaged me. I could not have been happier when I heard
that Dominic Crossan had been designated and had agreed to write
the book. I had very much admired his work on the parables and his
role in the Parables Seminar, and especially the wider literary initiation and sensitivities he brought to these studies. After seeing the
typescript of the work I saw him at our annual meeting in 1979 and
told him how delighted I was with what he had done.

I particularly appreciated his decision to deal with my work in
biblical studies with joint attention to my writing in the wider area of
"theology and literature." This had its justification in the increasing
focus on language and rhetorics in our field. Even though my excursions into modern letters had not been directly related to biblical
scholarship, yet Crossan could rightly be interested—given the historical purpose of the series in question—in the wider humanistic

Apropos of John Dominic Crossan, *A Fragile Craft: The Work of Amos Niven Wilder*,
Society of Biblical Literature Centennial Series III, Biblical Scholarship in North
America 3 (Missoula, Mont.: Scholars Press, 1981).

Among those whose work is assessed in this series, I am in the happy situation of
surviving the publication. I am therefore able to record my appreciation of this attention to my writings and to carry further the discussion of those issues which have
concerned me, so discerningly appraised in Dominic Crossan's survey.—A.N.W.

orientation of workers in our discipline. More particularly he could find in both areas of my work a distinctive approach to imagery and language-media which had direct bearing on hermeneutics and on biblical theology.

Thus I could only be happy with Crossan's view of his assignment as he identifies it in his preface, not least with his proper intention to enter into dialogue with my views, in the hope "that by our inter-changes the weapons of both of us may be sharpened for further use on future fields" (p. 4). I also appreciate his concern "not to pull Wilder unfairly out of his situation and into my own." Though an older worker will always feel that those of a new generation can never enter into the vicissitudes of earlier decades as he himself has known them, yet Crossan has exhibited extraordinary probity and thoroughness in reporting and analyzing my disparate writings and reading them in context. This detachment yet sympathy is all the more remarkable since my own approach to literary criticism was until more recently so unformulated.

The title of the book, *A Fragile Craft*, cited from my translation of a poem by Hölderlin, may at first puzzle the reader, but only until he has read the author's prologue, "Fragility and Craft." In his inimita-ble way Crossan has invoked a gorgeous parable for the strategies of the imagination, Edgar Allen Poe's "A Descent into the Maelström." The discerning initiate survives his immersion in the demonic and the preternatural by shrewdly conspiring with their destructive furies.

At one level, no doubt, Crossan—by punning—applies this para-ble of the fragile but surviving "craft" to what may be seen as the venturesome strategy of my scholarly focus and academic pursuits. There have, indeed, been sometimes dismaying risks and liabilities for me as regards my professional role consequent on my heavy investment in literary or aesthetic concerns. These hazards of workers at the margins of our academic disciplines as well as in the market-place of scholarly appointment are familiar. The innovative or oddball scholar should be able to convince his colleagues and whatever appointive authorities that his input is germane to the discipline in question and that he commands that discipline sufficiently to share in the ongoing tasks of the field.

In my own case the issue arose most clearly in connection with my appointment beyond the seminary level at Andover Newton Theological Seminary to a university level in the Federated Theological Faculty at the University of Chicago. In the preliminary exploration at Chicago I recall that Ernest Colwell, dean of that faculty, pressed me with respect to this appointment in the field of the New Testament as to my long addiction to literary pursuits. The implication was that such a double vocation could only be at the expense of sufficient concentration on biblical studies. It happened that at this same colloquy Mervin Deems was being considered for appointment in the field of church history. I reminded Colwell and his colleagues that Deems had a notable asset in his proficiency with organ and piano, and I felt that my own case was similar. In the upshot I believe that my role in literary studies was appreciated as an asset in itself and one which could enrich my more specialized work both in the Divinity School and in the Department of New Testament and Early Christianity in the Division of Humanities in the University. It was perhaps not irrelevant that Colwell had himself at one stage been a teacher of English literature.

At another level Poe's parable of the "fragile craft," surviving the maelstrom, may be taken as a transcription of the experience of young Americans of my generation in World War I. "In the destructive element immerse" (Joseph Conrad). Especially as volunteers, many of us did indeed "dare the unpastured dragon in its den." If we did not emerge from the war like Poe's survivor with our hair turned white, yet we were changed. Crossan properly connects my later interest in eschatology and apocalyptic with this experience. But, more than that, like exsoldiers of other such world dramas, sharing a baptism unknown to our civilian contemporaries, we could not but feel—if only in self-defense in a world turned to "normalcy"—that we were a peculiar breed. As I wrote in the immediate sequel,

> Yet we who sensed the exaltations of war
> Enveloped in the Aeschylean mood
> From moon to moon, who knew the imminence
> Of unnamed powers, are returned therefore
> Children of storm, an earthquake-fostered brood,
> Dowered within the womb of great events.[1]

---

1. "Boanerges," *Battle-Retrospect and Other Poems* (New Haven: Yale University Press, 1923).

I only cite this no doubt juvenile reaction to our experience because it fits so well with Poe's analogue. I shall return below to the suspect issue of glamorizing war. Whatever deepening of awareness our passage through the maelstrom of war may have occasioned, certainly this brought no guarantee of wisdom. On the other hand Poe's analogue as Crossan evokes it may well stand for that initiation into a deeper reality which has overtaken the modern world as a whole, and of which World War I was only a part.

ESCHATOLOGY AND ETHICS
(pp. 9–25)

After his preface and prologue Crossan divides his survey of my work under three heads in a way which enables him to take account of chronological developments and of the interrelation of biblical and literary-cultural studies. The first such head or chapter, "Eschatology and Ethics," deals with my doctoral dissertation, and especially with its revisions as published in 1939 and 1950, *Eschatology and Ethics in the Teaching of Jesus*. As he notes, the original thesis had confined itself to this topic "as represented in Matthew." The basic conclusions of the thesis were carried over into the publications indicated though now the limitation to Matthew was dropped.

I felt that the modulation from Matthew to the historical Jesus was legitimate. In the original thesis I had all along highlighted the special horizon of Matthew and his formulations. I could now allow even more particularly for all such secondary overlays and use them as pointers to the older stratum. Especially in my 1950 revision I took account of the extensive authoritative scholarship of that period on the historical Jesus and his eschatological sayings. Granting the uncertainty of the original sayings and the fluidity of the tradition I felt that for the purposes of my particular inquiry, that of the *relation* of eschatology to ethics, I had good grounds for my conclusions. Here my main contribution, such as it was, was to illuminate the matter in terms of my understanding of the eschatological "myth."

Crossan is quite right to expose the problem here of an adequate discrimination of authentic Jesus utterance. He is more than charitable in passing over the paucity of strictly philological investigation in my writing. Yet I could plead that the sifted corpus of sayings of Jesus to which I appeal was drastically selected. That Jesus announced an imminent Kingdom did not carry with it for me either that he provided specifications as to time and manner or that he identified himself as Son of Man. Whether he spoke at all of the coming of the Son of Man I was then inclined to leave open. I was convinced that he spoke of the Kingdom as suffering violence from the time of the Baptist and followed Kraeling in referring this to the mythological powers of evil. Crossan's own sobered retreat from apocalypticism here is suggested by his assignment of Mark 1:15, "The time is fulfilled and the kingdom of God is at hand," to the evangelist and not to Jesus. No doubt Mark's sequel, "repent, and believe in the gospel," represents his own formulation, but the heralding of the Kingdom would appear, in the light of other sayings, to have been both original and central.

All in all my position as to the original core of sayings was much the same as that of the critical vanguard of the time, one that has not notably changed down to our own time, as one can judge by the more recent work of such scholars as Kümmel and Perrin. Crossan's critique arises rather at the point of interpretive approach. Taking his cue from the parables he urges that one should recognize that Jesus' eschatological sayings were also *sui generis*, and that their radicality properly excluded the kind of cultural meaning traditionally associated with the imagery. Just as we err in turning the iconoclastic parables into clichés, so we err in assigning univocal import to the "apocalyptic" media, as though Jesus was concerned to carry forward or to revise the mythological portrayal of history and its fulfillment shared by his people. It is my view that Crossan is right in insisting on the iconoclastic radicality of Jesus' teaching in both areas, but that he presses it so far as to be in danger of dehistoricizing the teacher. I shall return to this topic farther on.

In any case the issue, as Crossan rightly says, is one both of "corpus" and "commentary," sayings and interpretation. In the last analysis, even though as in my case the establishment of the corpus may not be exhaustively martialed, one finally comes down to an act of judgment. So far as concerns that major issue which is still before us, eschatology and ethics in the teaching of Jesus, I am content to rest my case on the material I cite with its implications.

It is another issue and one which Crossan rightly draws attention to, when, in company with Bultmann, I propose that "even supposing that our best hypothesis only presents us with a Jesus created by the tradition," yet our findings would still be relevant. Crossan sees this concession as an illogical abandonment of the prior focus on the historical Jesus. Here I would seem to be joining those who either out of historical skepticism or a theological-kerygmatic premise discount our efforts to go behind the evangelists. I agree with Crossan in his caveat. Like him I am concerned with the historical Jesus. My concession is, as he says (p. 15), "ambivalent." But in any case this is another and different issue. My investigation is directed to the historical founder. I believe that a persuasive historical judgment can be made about his teaching in the area in question. For those who see in the records mainly a community product and a testimony to its later views I would urge that even so there is a latent continuity. The horizon in which we assess the days of Jesus' ministry must include the responses of his followers all along the line of the emerging movement he initiated.

Here is an issue about biography and historiography which I would like to pause over. Crossan seems to me to have too punctiliar a view of agency and transactions in an historical movement like that in which Jesus was involved. One seeks of course to distinguish the actor and his peculiar input from his antecedents and his succession. One seeks to isolate an initial phase, even the *novum*, from its sequels. But there is a certain positivism that may operate here. We are already aware of this danger in our current dissatisfaction with "the criterion of dissimilarity" in identifying the *ipsissima verba* of Jesus. It seems to me that Crossan may have too closed a view of the historical "core," thus truncating it from its original implications and from those modulations ("plurivalencies"!) which surface in the tradition. Jesus' vein of utterance, as I have remarked elsewhere, could "breed" no doubt "secondary" sayings which nevertheless testify to his originality.

This does not mean that we should not seek to distinguish between authentic and secondary sayings, nor of course between Matthew and the historical Jesus. But it does mean that there is a latent continuity which so far as it can be identified will enrich and confirm what we know of him in our oldest strata. If Crossan has too punctiliar a view here, it is no doubt related to his radically iconoclastic understanding of Jesus vis-à-vis his setting. On this view any transmission of his words that takes on the character of domestication to the situation of his followers can only be a betrayal. But behind whatever intrusive motifs, pragmatic or ideological, which we may see as secondary, we should not lose sight of the original shaping vision whose dynamic still operates. This also makes up a part of our documentation of the historical Jesus.

For an analogy I point to the familiar *topos* of the delay of the Parousia. We used to suppose, and many no doubt still do, that this postponement occasioned a crisis in the early church, one which determined many sweeping changes in its theology and structure. But this was to misconceive the mythical outlook and to literalize one feature of it. With rare exceptions with which we are familiar, the teleology of the movement adapted itself to the ongoing of time, and its dream of consummation found other categories for its expression. But these still testified to the original world-changing vision. Again, we do not have continuity in "common ideas and terminology," but we have one in what underlies these. This distinction as it bears on the Jesus-tradition troubles Crossan (pp. 16–17). But where we have modulation of the terminology, related to changing milieu, we should attend not only to the new formulations but to the continuity, the trajectory, which is operative, and this instructs us as to the prior and governing perspective.

So far as concerns our ongoing task of interpreting Jesus' outlook in its relation to ethics, there are two main issues, as it seems to me, which come to the fore in Crossan's discussion of my work. One has to do, again, with the "corpus" or selection of the evidence and the resulting image of Jesus and his mission. The other has to do with our interpretation of his language and symbol. With respect to the first Crossan is conscientiously reticent in imposing his own views and confines himself largely to queries and challenges. Nevertheless one can recognize here a certain stance which determines both the image of the Nazarene and the corpus of his sayings and deeds. His position appears to represent one pole of an old ever-fluctuating swing, though in a new context. It is a question of how far Jesus' outlook was determined by apocalyptic-eschatological vision and categories. Here Crossan would appear to join those who would now discount the regulative importance of such mythical ideology. For him we see here a very "unapocalyptic" kind of eschatology.

The contemporary context of this discounting of the views of Schweitzer and Johannes Weiss and others is an interesting one. Those like Crossan who today have a heavy investment in the study of the parables of Jesus tend to find their focus at this point. Instead of reading the parables in the light of other strains of his teaching, prophetic and eschatological, they reverse this procedure. Instead of determining the authentic corpus in the light of his eschatological outlook and sayings, they find their orientation in the parables. Of course there is justification for this within limits. We know that secondary features of the eschatological and apocalyptic scenario were assigned to Jesus in the course of the transmission of his sayings. Even as regards the parables, a good number of these were mistakenly related to the Kingdom. More decisive, however, has been the conviction that with the parables we find a Jesus unmistakably at home in the empirical reality of his setting. Along with this goes the wide agreement, based also on literary-generic considerations, that in the parables duly reconstructed we have the best authenticated survivals of his utterance.

On the other hand, the difficulty scholars have had in reaching agreement about the eschatological sayings has discouraged us about their original form and import. The fact, also, that this ambiguously otherworldly vein in his supposed teaching was later seen as dogmatized, and led in the history of the church to such confusions and betrayals of the faith, has prompted a resort to the less mysterious Jesus revealed to us in the stories and aphorisms. Thus we can appreciate the capsule summary of Robert Funk: The Christian movement began with parables. After a long history both in the church and in scholarship of concern with myth we are returning today to the parables!

It is my view, however, that Jesus' eschatological vision and announcement were determinative in his mission, and that the parables, recognizing their differences, are to be read in this light. This is, of course, a matter to be argued in scholarly terms. But first it can be urged that all such narratives or tropes as the parables, for their right understanding, rest on prior assumptions. As Ricoeur has said in this connection, the meaning of a story presupposes a larger story. Those who would interpret the parables of Jesus for themselves and apart from the eschatological horizon in terms of which he lived and spoke must needs invoke *some* prior assumption or world-story or "ontology." Indeed, those like Crossan would tend to identify such an ontology, radically iconoclastic, with Jesus' own basic orientation. Thus the meaning of the parables would serve as a criterion by which to assess and sift whatever mythological teaching may be assigned to him.

We are thus led back to the historical question. I believe that we have more direct evidence of Jesus' eschatology and world-story in the records than can be found in the parables. Even if we are unsure about his eschatological sayings we need to formulate his historical-cosmic outlook as best we can to locate his orientation. We do not have a sufficient base in his stories. One major consideration here is the very nature of Israel's dealing with reality. In Israel's world-vision the particulars of story and recital are always inseparable from a determining dogma, a mapping of the course of the world under the providence of God.

I believe that Jesus was heir to this tradition. His categories for dealing with time and history were drawn from it. Communication with his audience and generation required it. The crisis of his hour, both cultural and political, evoked a radical formulation and intensified symbol for Israel's hope and calling. Whether we call this eschatological message "apocalyptic" or not is a matter of words. We cannot well locate Jesus' outlook without taking account of his predecessor, John the Baptist, or of the time-sense of his followers. Most important to keep in mind is that "good news" or "salvation" or "fulfillment" implied totality and finality, as in the case of Deutero-Isaiah's version of the national hope. This required cosmic-dramatic language for its announcement. The decisive theocratic operation of God with its world-implications of judgment and renewal in the public theater of history could not be conveyed by parables and aphorisms alone. These could only enforce and exemplify the wider event and drama.

Of course some of the parables themselves warn of judgment and suggest rewards and punishments. Some open out future and promise. But these need to be correlated with Jesus' world-symbol and eschatological myth—with his choice of twelve disciples, his challenge to

Jerusalem and the Temple, his wrestle with Satan and the demons who from the days of John the Baptist assail the Kingdom, with his proleptic celebrations of the eschatological or messianic feast, together with his expectation of the Kingdom if only in the Lord's prayer and the Beatitudes. The parables enforce the concreteness of the drama, the apocalyptic symbol assigns it cosmic and total character. I do not know just what eschatological sayings Crossan would include in his own "corpus" of authentic utterance, but this wider vein of Jesus' message provides a necessary context for our understanding of his stories and mission.

But here arises the second main issue, as I see it, in Crossan's discussion of my work. It has to do with the interpretation of all such symbol. How do we come to terms with such mythical mentality and language? Crossan agrees that we should not read it literally or aesthetically. I urge that it is anachronistic for us to apply to such visionary speech our own distinctions of symbolic and literal. I urge that this kind of knowing and representation is naive, a kind of registering of reality which is dynamic (like a spell or vision). The picturing is immediate and autonomous, so that there is no question here of deliberate symbolizing. This kind of plastic perception need not be thought of as abnormal or arbitrary. It is analogous to that novel grasp or insight associated with a "live metaphor." But what I am concerned to safeguard here is the aspect of predication or testimony in the visioning, which while it is not discursive or literal is nevertheless reportorial in its own kind. At stake here is the truth-value of the imagery and poetics of Jesus' world-vision and history-vision in its relation to those of Israel.

Crossan is right in saying that all this discussion of symbol should be grounded in a more sophisticated analysis of language. But he appears to misunderstand my use of the category "naive" in associating it with "the playing child" and in asking how it fits with "the mind that created the parables" (p. 42). What really troubles Crossan here, I believe, goes deeper, and that is his "sophisticated" view of language as nonreferential. Where I find "meaning" in Jesus' world-picture and time-picture, where I find valid orientation and reality-reference, he, if I am not mistaken, would wish to relativize all such figuration and go behind it to a deeper level where all such world-making is generated.

LITERATURE AND THE BIBLE
(pp. 27–53)

In this second part of the book Crossan scans a long period of my writing during which assessment of modern letters alternated with biblical studies. The focus was on Christianity and culture, but this inevitably led back to the Scriptures. Not only were the pristine voices of the canon themselves culturally determined, but the vicissitudes of our modern hermeneutic both within and outside the church have been conditioned by the cultural context. My own long wrestling with modern letters was motivated not only by concern for the continuing normative authority of the Bible. In my view these literary studies also illuminated the texts themselves. Adequate biblical interpretation calls for the widest possible command of comparative literatures and language phenomena but also for initiation into the richly human apperceptions and horizons disclosed in them.

Going back to my first book dealing with literature, *Spiritual Aspects of the New Poetry* (1940), Crossan notes my recurrent use of the pejorative category "negation" in assessing the writings. Though from time to time I defend this trait in our disabused authors over against any superficial affirmation, yet I recognize today that this epithet was simplistic and judgmental.

While one might wish to justify ultimate appraisal of a work as nay-saying or yea-saying I learned later that one must do so only in terms of its total structure and context. The case is like that of pornography or blasphemy and their discrimination. One can compare John Gardner's test for a "moral fiction." Thus I find no difficulty in extolling what may at first seem the "negation" in the work of Samuel Beckett. Some would identify affirmation and health in the work of even the most nihilistic artists in view of the fact that they still go on with their work. More to the point is what we see in Beckett, in whose case the probing of darkness and meaninglessness manifests such tenacity, such freedom from self-pity and such a dazzling gamut of strategies. An improper "negation" is featured rather by evasion, sentimentality or a lust for demolition.

A more fundamental and more interesting issue arises here—indirectly raised by Crossan—as to the propriety of a "Christian discrimination" vis-à-vis the arts. We heard a lot about this kind of approach in the thirties and forties. It was only later, here again, that I learned to justify it as but one among other commonly admitted stances in cultural appraisal. This position recognizes that properly speaking there is only one organon of criticism, but that it can be illuminated from differing perspectives. Thus that seemingly dogmatic criterion with which I operated somewhat simplistically needed to recognize that any such approach should be continually open to correction from other perspectives. Such criticism, moreover, should be fully appropriate to the medium in question and therefore where literature is involved should relate to language considerations. Clearer awareness of this came to me only later in my work.

With these qualifications, however, I would still hold out for a "Christian discrimination" in dealing with literature and the arts. Whether it is welcome or not, however suspect it may appear in the forum of secular criticism and aesthetics, here is the peculiar thrust and horizon whereby the initiated theologian can introduce neglected insights into the common task. These challenges should not dogmatically shortcut the operations of appraisal but deal with all levels of literary and linguistic criticism by attention to their methods and assumptions. A special resource here is that unique repertoire of literary modes, the language-world of Scripture, which opens up neglected dimensions of the arts of communication.

The current agenda in "religion and literature" in its concern for new sophistications and interdisciplinary enrichment has widely bracketed or neglected the tasks of a Christian or theological discrimination. Much as we can learn from secular criticism and secular texts we should not be only on the receiving end in these pursuits. Why should the religionist or the theologian enter this arena with one arm tied behind his back? The Marxists, the structuralists, the aestheticists have not thus handicapped themselves.

Crossan, indeed (pp. 31–32), locates one area in my cultural assessment where my own stance is certainly vulnerable, namely my youthful response to my experience in World War I. In my book of poems, *Battle-Retrospect*, and in later work I testify to "the prestige of the war experience and its imaginative overtones." These poems reflect a kind of war nostalgia which can well appear scandalous. This matter of my seeming glamorizing of war is worth looking at for a moment. What is interesting to me about this quasi-obsession (which among some veterans has taken the form of a war-psychosis) is that it was inseparable from that whole experience of ordeal which later threw so much light for me on early Christian apocalyptic. It was not that the horrors of war were ignored but that the scale of events dwarfed all other considerations.

Nevertheless, the following considerations are relevant. (1) Most of these verses belong to what are usually referred to as "juvenilia." (2) Though after months of ambulance driving I was a combatant in the army itself for a considerable period in the field artillery, I had no experience of frontline infantry service. (3) The imaginative reactions of youth in this hyperdramatic theater could well dominate more realistic considerations. (4) Any illusions in my transcription of "Armageddon" should be weighed in the scale against the cynicism and irresponsibility which prevailed so widely in the sequel. It was not altogether inappropriate, finally, that with whatever blinders a comrade-in-arms should maintain the worth and defend the contributions of those of his generation who gave their lives in "Woodrow Wilson's war."

So when Crossan asks—apropos of my poem "Armageddon" about the Soissons offensive of July 1918—"What has Soissons to do with Patmos?" I could reply that even this postjuvenilia poem (1928), as in some sense "war poetry of affirmation" (p. 32), had its theological justification. Restraints on evil take different forms in different conjunctures.

This issue could lead us far. It is one thing to glamorize war; it is another to recognize a valid mythology of devotion and sacrifice, even in clouded causes. Crossan's appeal to "Patmos" suggests that all Utopian ventures in history for Christians should be spiritual and nonviolent only.

But this touches on the very raison d'être of my book on eschatology and ethics. This study oriented to Schweitzer's categories was not undertaken only as an historical investigation. Immediate problems for the churches in those decades had to do with the relevance of the Gospels for modern ethical issues, the modern bearings of the Sermon on the Mount, and the obligations implied in the imitation of Christ.

To take the issue of nonresistance in its bearing on public authority, certainly one upshot of the study was that the context of Jesus' teaching and example was such that applications in this area were not mandated for his followers in later contexts. In Schweitzer's view this is clear enough in his view of the injunctions as "interim ethics." While I did not accept this understanding of the sayings I did hold that they were specially conditioned by the circumstances of his mission and its eschatological horizon. Our own later obligations as Christians while deeply instructed by those precedents have to be worked out creatively with the guidance of the Spirit in the light of our own situation.

This is all familiar, and I take it that Crossan would agree. This is not the place to engage in a debate about political ethic, but there is one issue raised by my no doubt adolescent reaction to the war which calls for comment here. As an older survivor of that generation I often find it difficult to communicate about our experience with the mind-set of today's liberal-minded intellectuals and churchmen. Their understandable disabusement with political and patriotic clichés and their contagious myths of liberation have made it almost impossible for them to put themselves in our places in that now long-gone scenario. It is not a question of wishing to whitewash that war or any war. It is a question of basic political consciousness. Among our moderns there has been an erosion of the basic presuppositions of *politeia*, of the primordial bonding and cement which are the substructure of society, the grounds of legitimacy. The suspicion of authorities reaches to authority itself.

With these premises it is not surprising that my apparent romanticizing of my war experience should occasion surprise. There should be no condoning of war or Caesar or violence. But in World War I with whatever oversimplifications many of us saw our role as that of establishing legitimate authority in a world of nations moving away from anarchy toward law, structure and courts. Those who would demur should at least make clear how they understand the viability of clan and polis. There is no intrinsic distinction between the constable in the local neighborhood and the due restraints of violence in city, nation and world.

In my *Eschatology and Ethics* I recognized special forms of mission and witness determined by circumstances. Today they have their analogies in special vocations and in the witness of such disciples as those found in the peace churches. But there is nothing in either of the Covenants which disallows the primordial structures and legitimacy of societal order and authority. Paul recognizes these in Romans 13[2] and in his appeal to Caesar before Festus. The due functions of Caesar and of the tax-gatherers were taken for granted in Jesus' sayings and activity.

Crossan's recurrent query as to my way of interpreting the mythological imagery in the texts—as neither literal nor symbolic but "naive"—appears again in this second chapter. In the first chapter where it is a question of understanding the eschatological sayings in their first-century context my point had been that they were "naive" in the sense of visionary. These representations of "world" and time and agency were, indeed, fictive yet involved real perception and real predication related to Israel's inherited world-story. In that particular context Crossan questioned my category of "naive" as not radical enough. In his view Jesus' eschatological perception and sayings were more subversive than that and disallowed any portrayal or charting of the world's course.

In this second chapter, dealing with "literature and the Bible," and with Christianity and culture, the same queries arise now with respect to the wider context of eschatological myth and its modern implications. Where I would wish to validate a reading of world-history in terms of the "real time-sense and hope of early Christianity" (p. 43) or of "the total story of Paradise Lost and Paradise Regained" (p. 50), he would disallow all such continuing relevancies of the ancient symbol. He believes that if one admits the relativity and obsolescence of details of the first-century myth—such details as "the clouds of heaven" or "the last trumpet"—one should also do the same with the basic and more total imagery as it bears on time, judgment and fulfillment (p. 43).

Crossan notes that I have approached such a more radical questioning of the apocalyptic categories especially in envisaging an eschatological mysticism in Jesus' outlook. He cites me (p. 43) as

---

2. I am surprised that Crossan (p. 59) in identifying naive and obsolescent elements in tradition should fix on Romans 13 as an example, in its bearing on "political and economic realities." Surely interpretation has learned to distinguish between Paul's basic recognition of the structures of civil authority—urged against antinomian charismatics—and "obedience" to the powers that be when they become abusive and idolatrous.

recognizing the "symbolic" and therefore dispensable character not only of details of the eschatological scenario but of its very premises. In my view, as he sees it, "the very *coming* is symbolic," and he cites my remark,

> We must frankly concede that no such dramatic return of Christ with the clouds is to be expected in the course of history. He has his own way of coming but not this way.

Also as regards the *time* category I had observed, "The kingdom of God is at hand—ever at hand, and in a degree ever within reach."

Crossan likes what he sees here as my concessions. He is understandably on guard against any reading even of the basic symbol which would unduly fix and stereotype its meaning, turn it into an ideology and thus limit its range of implication. He can formulate this in another way by urging the plurivalence of the language as against a limiting univocal rendition of it. But in my view something very important is lost if we go so far as to relativize and forfeit the basic categories and teleology of Israel's world-vision as these are repossessed in Jesus' eschatological imagery. Even when later cultural factors threaten to compromise them their control continues to operate in a crucial way, as we can already recognize in the changing thought-world of the Fourth Gospel. This Gospel does not subvert the gospel into a timeless mysticism or Gnosticism.

Today there are two factors especially which prompt us to discredit some of the primordial features of the biblical myth, structural pillars of its world view: (1) our modern *anomie* which relativizes all models of order, and (2) our new awareness of other world-cultures. These challenges, however, are not unprecedented in kind, and while they may call for reconsideration of our biblical chartings, they do not disallow the basic orientation. This orientation in existence is fatefully woven into the language of the Scriptures and its continuities in image and rhetorics. Here are the archaic structures and models long built into the human pilgrimage, and irreversible, which have enabled survival and fruition. Such motifs as sovereignty, calling, covenant, providence, and consummation, as we find them in Jesus' sayings or elsewhere in the early Christian texts, have an authority linked with the history of language and life itself. Though we may rightly wish to be on guard against enslavement to univocal language, yet to disallow or revoke the crucial predications of Scripture is to bring down that house of language and wisdom which has defined our being from of old and which is like a second order of nature.

IMAGINATION AND RELIGION
(pp. 55–67)

It is in this final chapter that the root of Crossan's queries about my hermeneutic appears. All along the queries have revolved about my understanding of Jesus' eschatological myth. In chapter I it was a question of its meaning for Jesus and his hearers; in chapter II, of its meaning for us today in its bearing on world-history. Now in this concluding chapter and context Crossan deals with it in terms of language and ontology. Again I note that he does not obtrude his own views or spell them out. But his queries and hints suggest his own approach and one can fill this out by other things he has written.[3]

To anticipate, I would say that the crux of our differences lies in the kind and degree of radicality we assign to Jesus' message and sayings, in our understanding of his iconoclasm. At one level it is a question of Crossan's well-known category of radical paradox and subversiveness in his reading of the parables and other sayings. At a deeper level this is linked with a "deconstructionist" view of language and discourse as always qualified by negation. This basic epistemological qualification of speech should be taken seriously, and I shall return to it.

The immediate issue, however, and the point where my interpretation of the texts appears most vulnerable, is that of Jesus' iconoclasm; it is that of continuity versus discontinuity. Crossan evidently finds me attenuating the novelty of Jesus' challenge both by my undue inclusiveness in the sayings I recognize as authentic and by my interpretation of the symbol. Thus I would seem to domesticate Jesus' outlook and see him as indulging not rebuking the preconceptions, the ideology, of his audience.

---

3. Especially *Cliffs of Fall: Paradox and Polyvalence in the Parables of Jesus* (New York: Seabury Press, 1980); "Stages in Imagination," in *The Archeology of the Imagination, Journal of the American Academy of Religion*: Thematic Issue (Dec. 1980) edited by Charles Wingate; and "Difference and Divinity," *Semeia* 23 (1982): *Jacques Derrida and Biblical Studies*, 29–40.

One point at which this issue appears earlier in the book (p. 51) is in Crossan's discussion of my chapter on "The Parable" in my *Early Christian Rhetoric*. At one point I note there (pp. 80–81) what would seem the incompatibility of such an artistic and realistic form as the parable with the visionary eschatological utterances. "We do not easily reconcile such fastidious concern with form with eschatological fervor and passion." Thus we may be led to conclude: "The Jesus of the parables is the true humanist; the eschatological Jesus is a cloudy visionary." And again: "We cannot but be surprised by the fact that such incomparable human and naturalistic and artistic portrayal of daily life should come to us from one who spoke out of an acute eschatological crisis . . . yet we have in the parables no stridency and no fanaticism" (p. 77).

Crossan cites this and adds: "Had that surprise been pursued Wilder would have had to distinguish between different modes of eschatological vision in order to locate Jesus' understanding more precisely among them." He then goes on to ask: "What type of eschatology is profoundly at home in realistic everyday normalcy and detailed secular description?" and, "Is there such a thing as an anti-apocalyptic eschatology and is that where Jesus might best be located?" (p. 51).

Evidently Crossan envisages here a very sobered kind of eschatological myth, what one could call a "decosmicized" eschatology—lacking, that is, in what he would see as apocalyptic clichés or univocal dualistic motifs. Such repudiation of transcendental media would correspond to that subversiveness which he identifies with the parables. Thus in both veins of utterance we would find corollaries of that radical iconoclasm which Crossan highlights in Jesus' mission, that appeal to an ultimate *metanoia* which he can associate with a "negative theology."[4]

We can agree with Crossan that the parables should guide us in our assessment of Jesus' eschatological sayings, whether their genuineness or their interpretation. The fact that, as he says, they are "firmly planted in daily life" should no doubt lead us to the corollary that the visionary symbol also should have its own kind of rootedness and cogency. But surely this does not exclude dramatic portrayal of

4. *Cliffs of Fall*, 10–11.

the Kingdom and its coming, or visionary motifs likewise fatefully interwoven with his people's historical expectations. Though the parables are indeed firmly planted in daily life, yet in them elements of extravagance and hyperbole correspond to the surrealism of the new-age portrayal.

We should indeed suspect apocalyptic stereotype in Jesus' reported sayings just as we are unsatisfied with commonplace in his parables. In both areas we should look for his renewing distinctiveness. But our current suspicion of apocalyptic should not lead us to discount Jesus' own repertoire of surreal symbol in terms of which he evoked the wider context of his mission. In this light even such borrowed visionary motifs as the angels of the heavenly court, or Satan fallen from heaven, would have been germane elements in his appeal and in no wise only matters of end-time curiosity or perfervid fancy.

I am happy to agree with Crossan that both Jesus' parables and his "myth," both his particular stories and his embracing figuration of world and history, will have been congruous. But Crossan sees both as determined by paradox. As in the parables "world" or reality is subverted, so he must dedramatize and decosmicize the eschatology. In both areas he is concerned to clarify the radicality of Jesus' thrust. I also wish to safeguard this originality. But I believe that this can be insured in the case of the parables by a less drastic procedure than Crossan's yet without falling into banality. Likewise the eschatological discourse can be allowed its own plastic octaves in a way which respects Jesus' distinctiveness and which need not be construed as either fantasy or ideology. After all, the stories of the parables require their larger Story, and it is this which the imminent eschatology provides.

As in all situations of cultural *anomie* Jesus was compelled to resort to unwonted modes of discourse, to hard sayings, to archaic categories—all by way of appealing to a deeper hearing and a shocked reorientation. Only so could meaning be recrystallized out of delusion and meaninglessness.

If we recognize that Jesus' parables, as well as his aphorisms and his whole deportment, represented this kind of shocking witness, we may say the same about his eschatological categories and media. But here too, as in the case of the parables, the novelty and the surprise lay in their determination by the actual, the ordinary, the concrete occasion. The eschatological Kingdom which Jesus acclaimed and prayed for—like the Kingdom evoked in his parables—was masked but operative in the actual, the diurnal. What was new and subversive about it was that it was no dogma but a reading, a vision, of the empirical historical occasion in its ultimate context. Surprise and offense lay not only in the confounding parameters in terms of which salvation was acclaimed but in the pragmatic circumstance of the time and the ministry. The love, zeal and glory of God were exposed in the transactions of household, occupation, synagogue and temple.[5]

I can therefore agree with Crossan in recognizing that the parables should serve as one kind of control on our assessment of Jesus' eschatological outlook and sayings. Yet this does not mean that inappropriate criteria should be carried over and applied to this so different vein of utterance. If the parables were firmly planted in daily life, so, I would urge, were the transcendental sayings. If the parables were in various ways subversive, so was Jesus' version of the Kingdom. But the wider reading of God's operations in present and future required other kinds of figuration than that of the parables. That such mythos inevitably involved a kind of predication or portrayal of world and time only carried further the premises and implications in the parables themselves. The revolutionary word of Jesus would not have been Good News and would not, with full sanction, have evoked meaning out of disarray and confusion if he had not dramatized the ultimate, or, as we say, cosmological and ontological, coordinates of his historical work and ordeal. For these symbolic chartings of God's way with the world he was indebted to the long-obscured heritage of his people.

In Jesus' presence and words, then, we see a repossession and repristinization of Israel's covenantal archetypes, involving a public drama of loyalties and a wrestling of old and new. Despite the scandal, paradox and offense which were essential elements in Jesus' confrontation with his generation there was a basic continuity to which he appealed. Though we rightly seek to safeguard his originality and to dissociate him from authoritarian categories, whether of world view or morals, yet I am convinced that we must rec-

---

5. Here we have an analogue of God's promise in Ezekiel: ". . . there I will enter into judgment with you face to face" (20:35).

ognize the aspect of the *normative* in his discourse, a particular life-orientation in continuity with the past and transmitted to his followers.

Crossan deals with this issue of Jesus' iconoclasm differently. One should recognize what is at stake for him at this point. With his emphasis on the ontologically subversive character of the parables and other sayings he seeks to locate Jesus' impact at a creative level anterior to whatever cultural formulations and restraints. As with the parables, so with other "signs" of word or act, a "meaning" is identified which, while it may be enigmatic, is all the more fertile in implication. Thus the novelty and discontinuity in the sayings is of that same order as is evoked by Paul when he speaks of "the God who . . . calls into existence the things that do not exist" (Rom. 4:17). Here we can recall that Crossan has elsewhere suggested that "Jesus' paradoxality is the result of turning the aniconicity of Israel's God onto language itself, onto the very forms and content of human speech."[6]

Also at stake for Crossan in his view of Jesus' iconoclasm is the relevance of the Gospel for our post-modern crisis. Where I appeal to the mythical world-story and salvation-story which I see charted in Jesus' eschatology—answering to the *anomie* of his own setting—Crossan observes: "It is also possible that our twentieth-century world-loss is far more devastating than that of the first century, and that we shall have to accept many partial and incomplete versions instead of the one magnificently adequate one" (p. 25). Or again, where I look beyond our modern transitional disarray to a repossession of the ancient categories of meaning, he writes: "What if the great discontinuities, fissures and negativities of our period are not the passing prelude to new overarching certainties but are the *via negativa* of our transcendence, so that we presently need not greater positive certainty but greater negative capability?" (p. 61).

It is with this category of "negative capability"—unblocked receptivity and spontaneity—that we no doubt draw near to Crossan's main concern. We can further our dialogue with him by taking him seriously at this point. There are times when his formulations seem to lock him into a totally irrational position. The ontological reversal

6. *Cliffs of Fall*, 20.

which he ascribes to Jesus would throw his hearers back upon sheer enigma. "Meaning" in such a case could only be salvaged by way of some kind of nihilistic disclosure, located in an order of Otherness, a radical kind of spontaneity which nonetheless is only one more version of an all-too-familiar mysticism. Here there would be no orientation, no predication, no normativity in Jesus' language.

But Crossan is concerned not only with negative capability but with a negative dialectic. There are other contexts in which he recognizes that Jesus lent himself to positive statement and communication. Crossan is no less interested than the rest of us in locating the meaningfulness of Jesus' words for his own generation and their relevance for our modern crisis. Despite his appeals to subversiveness, paradoxality and negativity he also looks for some ultimate normativity of the Gospel. He recognizes that Jesus' speech was directed to particular hearers in a live communication to the ends of persuasion. Here one has only to look at his admirable discussion of the pragmatics, semantics and syntactics of Jesus' parables in his chapter "Parable and Metaphor," in *Cliffs of Fall.*

However disordered the language-world of his occasion, Jesus could not but avail himself of it for his message. The demands of intelligibility alone would have ruled out sheer enigma in his utterance, or total discontinuity with the language heritage of his auditors. Indeed, Crossan agrees with me that the novelty of the Gospel could not mean a total subversion of the language of the past. He cites with approval my observation that "the actual language-continuities of Christianity with its antecedents certainly limit the terms in which we can use absolutes or paradox about the new event of the Gospel" (p. 53).

Crossan seeks to manage his two contradictory postures by his category of negative dialectic. But he is not successful in bridging the gap between his view of language as on the one hand arbitrary, plurivalent, nonreferential, with "a void of meaning at its core," whose postulates therefore call for immediate annulment, and on the other hand as an indispensable social medium in terms of which we make our "worlds" for better or worse. His embarrassment here is no different from that of Derrida who recognizes that we have to work with the language and logics we have, however abusive we may suppose them. Derrida, for his part, draws back from that kind of total iconoclasm which, as he sees, could only end in the "monstrous." Crossan would appear to keep open a paradoxical ultimate, an order of apprehension beyond categories, an Absence within which God as the Other can act and speak. But the ontology presupposed here leads us to doubt whether we shall hear the voice of the Lord God of Sabbaoth or the occult echoes of an all-too-familiar Romanticism now *in extremis*.

To do him justice, Crossan wishes to safeguard the distinctiveness, the *novum*, of Jesus' speech against all betrayals of it by anemic cultural formulations and dwarfed categories. The world-transforming words (in the sense of *fata*) and ciphers, the *miraculum* of the Gospel, were not capturable in common parlance, and their import must not be forfeited by the univocal ways in which his hearers or ourselves have sought to construe or appropriate them. In the order of ontology this points to a preontological ground or fertile nihilism. In the order of language it calls for paradox and riddle. In the order of theology it mandates a negative theology. Yet in his analysis Crossan sees himself working as a historian. As is clear in the case of the parables, it is not on the basis of a premise but on that of scholarly method that he finds Jesus calling his hearers back to ground zero. In his view this iconoclasm more than compensated for any loss of "world" by opening up the potential of wonder.

With respect to Jesus' sayings, however, there must have been some substantial appropriation and continuation of the language of the past and its meaning, however iconoclastic his use of it. Where is the continuity? The issue lies here. I myself see a continuity at the level of denotative symbol and conception which Jesus both exploited and revisioned. We have a revolution of images. Crossan is more radical. The continuity he recognizes is preconceptual, precultural. Any continuity between Jesus and his antecedents or his followers is, as it were, underground. It lies at the level of "negative capability" or original virtuality or openness to the workings of God, that level which Crossan evokes in his interpretation of the parables.

But this view of meaning or relevance or normativeness of Jesus' words for his hearers or for his followers is so unworldly that it provides no orientation. Crossan is so intent on a prenoetic stage of the Gospel that even Israel's prior structuring of existence seems to play no part in it.

At several points in this third section Crossan appeals to some of my own writings which would appear to support his own radicality. In my discussion of apocalyptic rhetorics[7] I stress the alien and pre-cultural character of the language of such texts. Meaning has to be sought outside of current categories and media. Yet I noted that in the case of Jewish apocalyptic the acute crisis of symbol led to a recourse to older archetypal models. Though all the categories of reason and faith were confounded, Israel's seers, whether in the Books of Job or Daniel, found a grounding not in some aniconic mystique but in an older orientation which went back to the foundation of the world.

Crossan also cites one of my poems[8] in which I deal with death as negation, and in which I write that "the null-point/breeds new algebras," and that here we are "instructed by unreason." The null-point or zero thus represents the phase of negative capability or sheer virtuality which is open to miraculous disclosure.

> The null-point
> breeds new algebras,
> the ruin in nature
> proffers auguries.
> This hammer
> strikes sparks from the heart,
> the double-axe has its fulgurations.

Yet I would urge that even such transcendence and its unpredictable epiphanies similarly have their favoring context. Beyond the impasse or zero-point the ensuing "algebras" have their prior determinations, and their plurivalences are not gratuitous. Crossan is right that the factor of negation still attends upon all such figurations or predications. But here like some deconstructionists he appears to press a semiotic truism in such a way as to undermine the hard-won and irreversible achievements of our human exploration.

At the close of his discussion of the poem in question Crossan writes:

7. "The Rhetoric of Ancient and Modern Apocalyptic," *Interpretation* 25 (Oct. 1971): 436–53; also, *Jesus' Parables and the War of Myths* (Philadelphia: Fortress Press, 1982), 153–68.
8. P. 66. The poem, "A Hard Death," is cited from my collection, *Grace Confounding* (Philadelphia: Fortress Press, 1972), 26–27. First published in *Poetry: A Magazine of Verse* (Chicago) 107/3 (1965): 168.

One must certainly insist, as Wilder so eloquently has done, that both the zero and the algebras are necessary and that only in conjunction is either fully human. But by ignoring some safer line claiming that old algebras breed new ones Wilder has made it possible to ask whether much of our western horror has arisen not from too much zero in our humanity but from too much algebra, especially where such algebra is mimetic of some absolute algebra above, behind, before or below it. (p. 67)

This passage again shows how much our modern crisis is at stake for the author in the whole discussion. Because of the risks of ideology he must disallow any naming or imaging of reality that can take on the character of the univocal. He is impelled, therefore, to recall and stress the ultimate negation which relativizes all our world-making. This is in keeping with his reading of Jesus' parables as radically subversive and paradoxical.

Like the rest of us Crossan knows that human beings have to orient themselves in existence and construct houses of language and live in them. For him, however, any such edifices of meaning, any plotting of time and destiny whether by myth or story, any scenario of judgment and salvation, any dramatization of good and evil: all such world-charting lies under the shadow of the negative, like the tower of Babel. All such languaging of reality represents a fall from Eden, at best one arbitrary fabulation to be replaced by another, at worst a prison-house of delusion which can only be dispelled by a radical subversion of the word.

A wiser procedure, however, would seem to be that of discriminating and valuing those ventures in language, those myths and stories, which have founded and sustained our world and which experience validates. Their continuity structures our life in time just as language itself from ancient epochs has been interwoven with human survival. The "negative" operates here, indeed, as criticism and judgment. But *this* negative, as an aspect of ever-renewed testing, has nothing in common with a semiotic or ontological premise. There are some kinds of world-divination, apprehension, exploration, in language, which are not thus subject to reversal, and which should be trusted and exploited. As Isaiah writes, "He does not call back his words" (31:2), and this does not apply only to his words of judgment but also to his words of founding and promise.

8

Parables and the Kingdom

It is because Charles Hedrick looks to the analogy of parable and poem, as imaginative fiction, in seeking to identify the power of Jesus' narrative parables that he is led to proposals which diverge from the modern consensus and which may well represent a salutary contribution to it. This approach undercuts any too pragmatic or too specific interpretation of the texts, either in the ancient church or in our own hermeneutic. He pushes this characterization of the sayings very far, to the point that any figurative or metaphorical intention in them is at least bracketed, not only as regards the Kingdom of God but any other kind of referentiality.

In the light of his thorough documentation of the ways in which the tradition construed these parables Hedrick can plausibly conclude that the church had soon forgotten or misconstrued their original situation and purport. For clues we are therefore thrown back on the texts themselves. As imaginative fictions they *may* have had a meta-

Comment on a paper with this title read by Charles W. Hedrick at the annual meeting of the Society of Biblical Literature, 1987, in Boston and published in the Seminar Papers of that meeting, pp. 365–93.

Summary. Hedrick's canvass of the diverse interpretations and framings of Jesus' narrative parables in our texts indicates that his followers had soon forgotten their original context and purport. Whether they were intended metaphorically is unclear. Whether indeed the original parables had reference to the Kingdom of God is also in question. But this leaves us with a quandary as to the continuity of the tradition. In view of the plurality of their interpretations, how could the original parables have been normative in the community?—A.N.W.

phorical character, but any such visionary horizon may elude our categories of figuration. Even those "triggers" in the narratives which point beyond banality should not be read as metaphorical as though they "gave away" some ulterior sense. So Hedrick concludes that "the tales of Jesus mean exactly what they say—and perhaps more."

What one could call the "minimalism" in Hedrick's view of the parables—taking us back to square one—can be serviceable as a move back behind the long sedimentation in our interpretations of the parables. We find a similar move to set the parables above interpretation and to respect Jesus' words as *sui generis* or enigma or paradox in Dominic Crossan. James Breech also fixes on the texts apart from or prior to contextual relevancies. Moreover, if one reads the parables as oriented to the dynamic eschatological vision of Jesus' mission their purport and horizon would transcend any kind of empirical reference.

Thus if some of the original parables either specifically or by implication evoked the Kingdom of God, the category of metaphor is inappropriate and too limiting. The category of metaphor implies too specific a meaning of the Kingdom as correlative. The category of "absolute metaphor" (Allemann), since it excludes any correlative or comparison, only takes us back to the text itself and "what it says."

But what the tales "say" involves us in communication and the familiar formula that in language A speaks to B about C, that is, some shared "world." So here would be the genesis and inevitability of all later interpretation as conceded by Hedrick himself in his phrase "and perhaps more." We can appreciate Hedrick's caution at this point. But if Jesus' parables evoked no ostensible metaphorical correlative, yet Hedrick would no doubt agree that the communication awoke some kind of significant *resonance* in the hearers. Such resonance or deeper acoustic would rest on a richer apperception than one that could be mediated by the more particularized referentiality associated with metaphor, or trope.

Hedrick and others are therefore right in bidding us to "stay with the text," and constantly to return to what it says. As the tradition moved to various and differing appropriations of the parables, reflecting changing interests and apperceptions, we should look for the continuing power and purport of the original narratives in these later and derivative retellings.

At this point, however, I would qualify Hedrick's conjecture that the early church had lost touch with and forgotten the original meaning of Jesus' parables, with their context, and was thus impelled to seek such various readings of them. I would urge that their original force and bearing continued in a kind of underground way in the memory of the community. I am struck with the fact that so large a repertoire of the parables in so relatively integral a state was passed down along with the varying ways in which they were construed. It seems to me that as today the reader of Mark's Gospel would have "heard" not only the evangelist's contemporary interpretation of the Sower but also the text itself, as though as oracle, which Mark so prominently rehearses for the sake of its own resonance.

Nevertheless, Hedrick's canvass of the luxuriant variety of ways in which the early and later circles presented, construed and framed the parables in the course of their dissemination highlights for us in an acute form the problem of continuity in the literary tradition of the early church and also that of the linkage of the movement with its founder.

This quandary takes us back to the original telling of the tales to ask what kind of normativeness was implied in their first hearing and for the sequel. This query is especially open if like Hedrick we question any metaphorical intention in them. If these stories were "free and creative fictional descriptions of Jesus' poetic vision of reality"— with only indeterminate implications of some ulterior reference—we may well ask how they could have set in train in the sequel a legacy of "hearings" faithful to their original orientation.

This question of the continuity of the dissemination with its source is directly explored by Dominic Crossan.[1] Here it is the very variety of the interpretations of the sayings from the beginning which point us not to any original normativeness but to their prior disclosure of "the divine immediacy." This primordial genesis of the sayings will have generated and penetrated the rich plurisignificant trajectories of the later interpretations.

But this category of divine immediacy, determining the paradoxality of whatever mediations of it, would appear to foreclose any clues to perspective or orientation in Jesus' imaginative fictions.

---

1. Dominic Crossan, "Divine Immediacy and Human Immediacy: Towards a New First Principle in Historical Jesus Research," *Semeia* 44 (1988): 121–38.

Surely the creativity associated with the divine immediacy will have been related to prior and profound apperceptions shared with his public, though often suppressed or forgotten. If we can agree that "the finger of God" is to be recognized in Jesus' transactions with history and in his utterance it is still a question of what kind of God. The divine immediacy and the human immediacy opened up by it would not be directionless as though the encounter were with some philosophical absolute.

If any such perspective and normativeness shaped Jesus' outlook we should, indeed, be able to identify them in his parables, in the texts themselves. This involves a deeper kind of referentiality than the kind we associate with metaphorical action and its correlatives. Our difficulties arise here from the need to employ such shifting terms as symbol and metaphor. The word "imagination" itself is hardly negotiable since it is so variously colored with aesthetic, Romantic and other situated implications.

I return to our texts and to what they "say" and to how they resonate for those who share in the apperceptions out of which they were spoken. These fictions have specific traits in their composition and vision which evoke a particular perspective, no doubt preconceptual, prepredicational and prenomistic, yet implicitly normative at that level.

They thus oriented the ways in which later interpreters in the community mediated them in new contexts, in ways which then involved more specific reference. At this stage the fictive dramas were married to actuality; the plastic scenarios and their roles, actions and vicissitudes were identified with current agencies and conflicts; in some cases the plot lines were historicized by typology and allegory. But this process of merging model and actuality, however pragmatic, remained powerfully controlled by the particular reality-sense and vision of the parabler.

To properly identify the distinctiveness especially of the narrative parables of Jesus and therefore their kind of normativeness we should look beyond their poetics, structure and *topoi*. We are pushed back upon an elemental phenomenology of narrative attentive to such basic assumptions as those related to human destiny, selfhood and agency, and associated apprehensions of time, world and causation. The theater of these stories has its own *sensorium* and parameters.

By comparison the stories told in other cultures differ greatly both as language-acts and with respect to their texture. In some, the oneiric has a large part, and much is gratuitous and nebulous. In others, the narrative patterns are repetitive, as though reflecting a timeless, stagnant or arrested order of life. In still others the personae and happening are subordinated to a didactic intention which "thins" the portrayal. In others, again, the *humanum* evoked, however lifelike and moving, is circumscribed and dwarfed in all that relates to horizon and potential by a low ceiling associated with fate and fortune. In any such fictive worlds, as compared with our parables, the human being is not disclosed in depth, and we are reminded of photographs that have not been fully developed.

It is not only that the parables have such sharp focus and that their action is so brilliantly illuminated, or that so much is conveyed with such economy of means. More important is the special repertoire of basic attitudes and motives which underlie the recitals. Here deeper registers of human bondedness and destiny are caught up in the transactions. The hidden springs of behavior identified with anxiety, wanting, seeking, obligation, offense, esteem and shame are here interwoven with and transformed by a distinctive teleological premise which points all, beyond fate and chance, to a resolution portrayed as harvest, assize, feast and festal assembly.

This version of roles, projects, entanglement and outcomes constituted a human scenario which, in conjunction with the actualities of Jesus' mission and illuminating it, communicated its own normative vision. Subsequent interpretations either of Jesus as parabler or of particular parables however various would perpetuate its basic orientation and assumptions in the community shaped by it.

Jesus' tales, therefore, in terms of their resonance and hearing, "said" and "meant" what could only have had a distinctive and particular purport and were thus neither paradoxical in the sense of excluding understanding, nor open to a gratuitous free play of signification. If, indeed, as seems likely, the later tradition rightly traced in some of them a correlation with the Kingdom of God, we can agree with Hedrick that it would have been in terms of imaginative evocation rather than metaphorical comparison.

If the original "world of the parables" had the proleptic and teleological thrust which I have stressed, this would correlate well with the eschatological perspective of Jesus' mission: on the one hand the mythical vision of the time and its ordeal; on the other hand searching vignettes of its issues in depth in daily life. This transcendent context of the original stories was carried over in various ways in their later framings and interpretations. If we can recognize any forfeiture of their original force and horizon it will have been in those cases where "wisdom" and protognostic ontologies intruded, with their reduction of the total gamut of empirical-historical *realia* and moralities of the great transaction.

9

Story and Story-World

What happened?
Tell us a story.
That's only a story.
Is that story true?
Is that the whole story?

Stories and storytelling have come recently to command a new kind of attention. This interest does not stop with tales but extends to all kinds of narrative and recital, indeed to narrativity itself as distinct from other kinds of discourse. We have long known what a large role fabling, saga and epic have played in various cultures but we have new reasons for scrutinizing it. On the one hand it begins to dawn on us that a story, a fiction, reveals more than we had thought. One can say that the story tells more than what the storyteller tells. On the other hand we are less assured today as to what we have learned to tell ourselves about life and the world in other kinds of discourse.

We had thought that a story was just a story. These happenings and adventures: somebody "made them up"! Besides, they always belong to some past. They are always told in a past tense. And what about the storyteller? In the case of many narratives the teller is unknown, or fictitious. Even the known author is something of a masque and

This chapter originally appeared in *Interpretation* 37 (Oct. 1983), Union Theological Seminary in Virginia, and is used by permission.

playactor. His persona is elusive. How does he know all this! All in all these stories of what happened may, indeed, be vivid but they are doubly removed like dreams the morning after. So we have valued all such fictions as engrossing but have assigned them to the world of make-believe.

But lately we have come to recognize that these stories were not made up out of whole cloth, were not idle fabling. These heroes and villains and their vicissitudes were not just dreamed up; they were in some sense dictated! These particular scenarios were not invented but were somehow imposed on the narrator. What happened and how things happened in different stories were determined by differing assumptions and values.

So today we look behind the fables and recitals and ask what shaped them. What climates fostered these various fauna and flora? Then we begin to realize that these fictions cannot be shut off in the past tense. These characters and plots have backgrounds which outlast them, orientations which continue to operate on us also. Behind all our different kinds of fabling there are overruling constellations, cultural and psychological, which reign over our imagination and preform our storying.

But our new interest in story is also related to recent inquiries into language itself. Narration is only one very ancient kind of communication among others. No doubt all the arts of speech from the earliest times served our forebears in their task of survival and the process of world-making. Beyond naming and signaling, various modes of utterance furthered their grasp of the world about them and enhanced human mutuality and communication. Along with such media as hymn, oracle and chant we cannot but recognize the all but universal form of storying we call "myth." The major function of this kind of recital through a long past rightly alerts us to the dynamic operations of other and more recent kinds of narrative.

Ancient tribes and city-states did not rehearse their fabulous origins to no purpose, nor tell the tales of their gods as idle distraction. By these as by their arts of ceremony they held the world together. In any kind of imaginative fabling we may well look for an analogous motivation.

Our contemporary interest in story has also been furthered by extensive analysis of folktales and of literary fiction. The current debates about historiography revolve about the borderline between record and fiction and the rights of imaginative reconstruction. But then we are impressed in a new way with the fact that great bodies of the world's literature and scriptures—not least the Bible—are so largely made up of story and narrative.

I

I leave these general observations for the present, however, to start at a different point and in the present. How is it that we account for the appeal of a story whether to children or grown-ups, for that which "keeps children from play and old men from the chimney corner" (Sir Philip Sidney)?

There is first of all a natural interest in, a curiosity about, happening, about *what happened*, especially if it was something unusual, something marvelous or creepy or ridiculous.

With this goes an interest in what happened *next*, and *next*, in how the recital unfolds. One is on a road and one wonders what is around the corner and about how the road forks.

But besides the interest in what is strange there is also an interest in what may be familiar, in *recognition*. Yes, we say, that is the way things are; that is the way things happen. That feature is lifelike; that detail is precisely evoked, exactly right.

There is also the interest in where the story *begins*. As the stage is set, and as the hearers are in expectation, out of all the innumerable possibilities of what could be recounted, what shall we hear about? When the silence is broken, where shall we find ourselves? The very first words of a tale come as surprise.

There is, moreover, the interest in the *end*. Beyond the interest in what happened next and next there is the interest in how it came out.

There is the interest, more or less conscious, in what the story *means*, in what the storyteller is "getting at."

Finally there is the interest in the *art of telling*, in the performance. Audiences appreciate virtuosity, mastery, dramatic skill. One can recognize this in their tacit or murmured responses, their Ohs and Ahs or Get on with it! or in their smiles and shudders.

It will be noticed that all these aspects of story are referred back to *interest*. This is cardinal. The first axiom of good storytelling is that it should capture and hold our attention. Whatever else they do, the teller-of-tales, the novelist, even the gossip, must "hold" their audience or reader. Otherwise the story is not heard to the end. If the hearer steals off, if the reader drops the book, if the television is turned off, then the telling is aborted, the story-world evaporates. A recital must capture attention, engage a varied register of responses, kindle and fuel dormant awarenesses, and maintain the hold of the fable to its end. But this driving power of interest says something about the disputed question as to the relation of fiction to reality, to which I shall return.

But this matter of engaging the interest of hearer or reader has other ramifications. Apart from the appeal of the narration itself—the scenario, the plot, the characters—there are other factors and strategies which nourish the power of the recital.

Important among these are what we may call the rituals of storytelling. The teller-of-tales from of old has always had something of the character of a charmer, and the initiates willingly enter into what they recognize as an artifice. They are happy to be transported. The world of a story is then like a special precinct and the history of fabling evidences the ways in which it is marked off, as well as the special features of the terrain. A story has its frame as well as its special rhetoric.

The situation in which a storyteller begins to "tell" always has some ceremonial character. A special kind of attention is aroused. There are recurrent formulas which reflect this. "Hearken!" "Behold!" ("Listen, my children and you shall hear. . . .") The tales themselves can begin with such conventions as "Once upon a time," just as longer rehearsals can be introduced by "In the beginning" or by invocations to the Muses or the Holy Spirit. In narrative cycles the fictive tenor is often maintained by sanctioning appeals or refrains as in the quaint old serial tale of *Aucassin and Nicolette*[1] with its recurrent rubric, "So say they, speak they, tell they the tale."

At the outset of the recital we may expect the bard or raconteur to gesture, to fix the auditors with his ("glittering") eye, and to adopt a heightened or urgent tone of voice suitable to the spell. We cross the threshold into the story-world. We can all remember from childhood

---

1. Thirteenth century. See among others the translation by Andrew Lang, various printings.

the hushed *incipits* appropriate to a tale of dark events: "Once upon a midnight dreary," or "It was a dark and stormy night." Similarly, when heads are put together for shared gossip and ears are greedy, we can recall the conspiratorial tone of the reporter. Thus all the tribe of Clio, whether historian or fabulist, Herodotus or Homer, scribe or troubadour, tale-teller or talebearer, all have their ways of captivating a willing audience.

Oral narrative inevitably assumes auditors at a special pitch of attention, and the tradition loves to stage the ceremony. So we get the troubadour standing before his liege and the assembled knights in the great hall at the feast; or we see the children sitting at the feet of the narrator by the family hearth; or anecdotes exchanged by the woodstove in a country store; veterans retailing their adventures and exploits at a reunion; or (as with Joseph Conrad) old sailors telling yarns of the sea and the jungle in some seamen's home.

One does not need to look far in the Bible to find examples of such ceremony in narration. In the Book of Acts Stephen, Peter and Paul defend themselves in their trials by recital of the gospel story, and the author loves to stage and formalize these hearings. Mark builds up the setting of Jesus' teaching in parables, thus lending a heightened tenor and acoustics to this vein of his teaching. Jesus challenges the imagination of his hearers with such rubrics as "Listen!" or "What think you?" or "With what comparison . . . ?" and voices the refrain, "He who has ears to hear, let him hear." Storytelling always partakes of theater, and it is not so far from such sacred examples to the modern colloquial spellbinder who begins, "You will not believe this, but let me tell you about so and so."

There are other ritual features of storytelling, whether written or oral, which contribute to the prestige of the story-world into which the reader or hearer is introduced. Though this realm is not the same as that of the lyric poem, they are not far apart. The storyteller and poet are both fabulists, and with the help of such signals as tone, rhythm, gesture and pace they usher us into a heightened world or another world. They evoke latent responses, richer senses and anointed eyes. They cast their spell. Magic claps his hood upon our benighted perception and we awaken to worlds unknown.

There are no doubt different degrees of all such sorcery. The world of an anecdote is not so far removed from actuality as that of a tale or a poem or a myth. But all tellers captivate our attention for their own fabled scenario, and thus take us out of ourselves more or less profoundly.

Since all such fabling narrative is so akin to poetry and so often merges with it, its power is well suggested by long-familiar tributes to poets and their transfigured worlds of the imagination. "Much have I traveled in the realms of gold," writes John Keats, referring to these worlds as he sees "their pure serene" manifest in Chapman's translation of Homer. The poets are accounted magicians, world-changers, dreamers of the true dream over against the tormented visions and phantoms of common existence. Wordsworth (if I may for ad hoc purposes cite unpublished lines of my own) was

> that grand
> Magician of the lakes who cast his spell
> Upon three counties so we cannot tell
> Even today if they be faery land,
> Some insubstantial annex of the earth,
> Or some cloud-continent where dreams have birth.

So too the storyteller dislocates and irrealizes our sense of time and place by invoking oneiric worlds or conjuring up never-never lands. Yet all such enchantment rests on some prior reality-sense and is penetrated by it. Just here is the issue to which all reflection on story and storytelling must come back.

II

I have been listing those aspects of a story which hold the interest of hearer or reader. I began with that universal human desire to know what happened. We want to be "in the know" about occurrences which affected others and which might have a bearing on our own circumstances and uncertainties. This may well be only an avid ear for "news," or anecdotes of local gossip. But it may extend beyond the immediate past to other episodes whose drama may likewise illuminate our situation.

Thus our interest in filling in what may be unknown extends even to remote antecedents. And here is an important point: this interest in whatever happened quickens our attention to both what we call fact and fiction. Both kinds of recital answer not only to our delight in being entertained but to some deeper demand to know not only what went on and what went before but also to know the patterns of all such transactions. Here it is a question of *how* things happen: the causes and connections and consequences. Even in fables and fictions these aspects may be strange, yet they involve us. These characters and their vicissitudes link up with our own predicaments, and their options and constraints, their entanglements and fortunes are familiar. Even tales of the marvelous are not only exercises in spellbinding, in thrill and shudder; they speak to our own wrestlings with necessity and fatality.

Thus our interest in what happened, as it motivates the appeal of a story, illuminates the appeal of every kind of narration. This profound interest, which is much more than curiosity, provides the motive for records and annals, as well as for legends and myths, and all such rehearsals of the past pass over into the story or stories of beginnings and their how and why. Our interest in what went before animates not only our particular stories but tribal stories and the world-story itself. But all such traditions and recitals, of course, have been shaped in various cultural contexts with their differing horizons. They have been orchestrated, so to speak, in diverse keys and with varying registers of social experience and of what was deemed important. As in ancient tapestries the weaving of all such fabulations evidences differing textures and motifs with differing threads, stitches and pigments.

In all such modulations we can recognize a common impulse. Human nature is prompted to probe and extrapolate on all its horizons, backward and forward, without and within. But it has a special zest in evoking antecedents, in contemporizing earlier vicissitudes and their configurations by story and myth. This also serves orientation. This also is a kind of charting of the way. (Is it too farfetched to think of the internalized memory which guides the flight patterns of migratory birds?) If, indeed, much of this storying is imaginative and fabulous we should not reproach it for departing from actuality and realism. We should rather recognize that daily life is itself mysterious and dynamic.

Though so far we have had oral storytelling specially in view, yet it is clear that much applies also to written narrative. Much of the world's written saga, gesta, epic derives, in any case, from oral antecedents, and bears the marks of their prior ceremonial acoustics and viva voce vivacity. In cultures at the stage of writing, of book and publication, it is true that the author indites his stories and histories for an absent audience. But this way of telling still reflects the special demands of story-world. Though now at a remove from the children or tribesmen or circles addressed, the narrator must find modulated devices to capture and hold the attention of the reader. Here the kinds of interest we have already listed still operate.

The special strategies of the novelist have been exhaustively studied in our time but it would lead too far to pursue these here. For our purposes it is enough to point to those fundamentals which link oral and written recital. The novelist is also some kind of charmer. He or she also takes the reader across a threshold and appeals to a special kind of expectation from the outset, if not by gesture and heightened tone of voice now by corresponding signals challenging attention to a tale. Before we begin reading we are alerted, if not by the very format of the book and its jacket, by the title page. Here we are already launched into a fiction by an intriguing title often qualified by such pointers as "a novel," or "a romance," or "a mystery." The fictional mode of older novels was suggested by such titles as "the history of" or "the adventures of" so-and-so. Sometimes the narrative is ascribed pseudonymously to a prestigious ancient or to a long-lost journal or letters, or even to recovered golden tablets or secret archives.

The very first words of such narrations, all the more under the disguises of realism, take us into a fictional scenario by all but unconscious modulations of tense, voice, person, tenor and style. We are beguiled by familiar signals into a theatrical action which exerts its spell. And here too, as in oral tales, the ensuing weaving of storied experience must maintain its sway over the imagination by a combination of surprise (novelty) and familiarity (recognition). Again, also, as in oral stories, the reader delights in the arts of the telling, and this means much more than style, rather a whole arsenal of resources and resonances. Finally, again as in an oral setting, the reader even at this distance from the author, should feel himself or herself a tacit interlocutor in the performance, a participant in the world-making going on.

III

At many points in this exploration we have been led to ask the overall question, not as to this or that story but as to narrativity itself. Among all the various modes of discourse what is its special function in the history and uses of language? This question goes deeper than that of the distinction between fiction and history, supposed as non-fiction. Both fall under the head of recital. We have seen that narration can include such different kinds of accounts as myths, folktales and parables, but also anecdotes, eyewitness reportings, annals and histories. Common to all, with their varying agendas, is a kind of serial rehearsal of lived experience, recalled or supposed, sequences whether remembered or imagined. Yet here we should bear in mind that just as imagination shapes actual memory and factual recollection, so empirical experience enters into even our most fanciful fabling. Our interest here is in narrativity itself. In any case the earliest narratives took no account of such distinctions.

One can well begin by asking why human beings tell stories and why they told stories in the first place. Communication has always offered other options. If one looks back to the earliest epochs, story-telling and fabling would seem unlikely occupations measured by the dire exigencies of human circumstance and the struggle for existence. No doubt all the arts including those of speech emerged out of some pragmatic relation to living. Our ancient predecessors oriented themselves to the unknown and to the jeopardies of life by differing conventions and media. If this appears in ritual and custom, in tool-making and building, in music and dance, it will also have been true of the uses of speech.

If one looks at the survivals and tablets from early eras one can find those of some societies in which oracles, hymns, incantations, codes abound but without saga or annals. Even where memorials appear they may be confined to the barest lists of rulers. The point is that the history of human consciousness does not always reflect the impulse to narration. Should we not say that this is one kind of ordering of existence which, going beyond other media of communication, served a richer grasp on it? Paul Ricoeur in his *Symbolism of Evil*[2]

---

2. (Boston: Beacon Press, 1969), 9 and *passim*. The sequence or archaeology is both historical and phenomenological.

has identified one sequence in the history of language in which exclamation, "avowal," appears to have preceded the myth. Here it was
only later that story emerged to articulate the inchoate, to provide a
landscape for the cry.

If one is thus led to speak technically of the "phenomenology" of
story must one not say that it is inseparably related to our sense of
time, and orientation in time? The more acute our awareness of time
and change and of what Eliade calls "the terror of history," the more
we are impelled to locate ourselves in the flood of succession, to
grasp at antecedents and establish connections with what has gone
before. It is not enough for memory to expand the transient present
by recall; it must structure this impermanence, and place us in this or
that reassuring pattern or chart or story which can thus also illuminate the present and the future.[3]

The impulse to narration therefore is deeply rooted. Its urgency of
course varies in different contexts. But even casual anecdotes or idle
tales whose appeal is that of entertainment carry over something of
what deeply concerns and involves us in more fateful kinds of narration. All stories have their presuppositions. But with the more significant kinds it becomes clearer. These all posit a scheme or order in
the nowhere of the world. From the first words of the story a scene
and a horizon are established and a succession in time, all in relation
to hearer or reader. We are alerted by such prefaces as "once upon a
time . . ." or "now it came to pass . . ." or "in the beginning . . . ,"
alerted to a world-making in process. We are glad to lend ourselves
to its persuasion because though it may be fictive it answers to our
gropings and lights up our obscurities and confusions.

---

3. In T.S. Eliot's *The Family Reunion* (New York, 1939), the concern of the protagonist, Henry, to understand the web of "happening" in which he is caught is central to
the play.

> I feel an overwhelming need for explanation. (p. 73)

> We do not know what we are doing . . .
> What is happening outside of the circle?
> And what is the meaning of happening?
> What ambush lies beyond the heather
> And behind the Standing Stones? . . .
> And what is being done to us?
> And what are we, and what are we doing? (chorus, p. 128)

We may seem to be going far afield in thus seeking the deeper motivation of storying and narrativity. Its importance, however, can only be seen when we relate it to our empiric human quest for orientation. By narrative we seek to orient ourselves in our experience of temporal succession and memory. To put this special function of story in context we may well remind ourselves that other arts serve the general task of orientation in other ways. The plastic and graphic arts, for example, are first of all spatial. Where narrative has sought to bring extension in time under control these arts have furthered the task of world-making by bringing extension in space under control. By marking, shaping and building they articulate the nontemporal plane of our being, with special reference to sight and touch. Iconography serves the reality-sense of peoples before it becomes associated with narrative.

Yet in recognizing that narrativity like all the arts has a basic relation to human orientation and the mapping of experience, we must still take account of the vast differences in the spectrum of all such figurations. While the genesis of storytelling is serious not all stories are equally serious. While myths and rehearsals were evoked in the first place like shelters to provide us with a habitation in whatever homelessness may attend the mortal creature, yet on other occasions narration is less fateful. Much of the world's treasury of fable and fiction appears to have been inspired by sheer delight in the play of fancy. Yet even such gratuitous excursions and imaginative worlds, like dreams, have their latent connections with what we call reality and testify to varying urgencies.

IV

In all these foregoing observations I have been sounding various features of story and narrative preliminary to the basic question as to their relation to what we call reality, the relation of fabulation to actuality, the relation of story-world to real world. If we are prompted to look back and ask what happened and what went before and how and why, then the question arises, Is that only a story? or Is that a true story? or Is that the whole story? or What does that story mean? These questions which children may ask about *Alice in Wonderland,* and which we may all ask about the Bible and Homer, or about *Don Quixote* and *War and Peace*—these questions point us to the various levels of correspondence between story and life, between imagination and the real. Even history as narration, with its more empiric probing of circumstances and causation, floats in this same ambiguous world of fabulation but is governed by the same urge to map our being and to know who we are and where we stand.

Granted that our modern outlook leads to a certain disparagement of all make-believe yet we also recognize that storying represents a kind of exploration. The storyteller does more than organize his tale and plot. His fable responds to and organizes an inchoate fund of longings, anguishes, obscurities, dreams. His narrations orchestrate, as by so many rehearsals and trial runs, our most urgent impasses and gropings. The story holds us because it lights up our own adventure. Fictions do not take us out of time and the world. Their sequences and vicissitudes are woven of the same contingencies, surprises and reversals which attend on our own uncertainties. Even tales of the marvelous do not take us out of the world. Magic and miracle reflect our wrestling with the bonds of the usual and with fate and limitation, and transcribe the wider order of possibility which haunts our necessities.

But just what is then the relation of story to real life? Of course some stories are more realistic than others. Yet even realistic stories are fictive, and their invented plots and scenarios take us out of our everyday world into their own story-world.

One view is that a story is "just a story," meaning that it has no special relation to life except as a diversion. Another common opinion is that a story is an imitation of life. But this only means that certain particulars in it correspond to our experience in the real world.

If we ask a prestigious body of modern critics about the relation of story-world to real world, they will reply that it is a false question. For one thing the story goes its own way and takes us with it; the storyteller is inventing not copying. He weaves his own web of happening and the meaning of every part and detail is determined by the whole sequence. We lose our place in the story if we stop to ask what this feature means or refers to outside it.

But, more important, these students of language will ask us what we mean by "real world." There is no "world" for us until we have named and languaged and storied whatever is. What we take to be the nature of things has been shaped by calling it so. This therefore is also a story-world. Here again we cannot move behind the story to what may be more "real." Our language-worlds are the only worlds we know!

We should take seriously this questioning of what we suppose to be real. Our mapping of it in language is no doubt conventional and suspect. If we talk about the "real world" in connection with stories we should recognize that in depth the really real is mysterious, elusive and inexhaustible. In one of his fictions Samuel Beckett explores it as the "*Unnamable.*"[4] He does this by mocking all our brainwashed versions of it. But by his persistent sardonic wrestling he rebukes those language-philosophers who say there is no world *except* language world. They push too far their valid insight that stories evoke their own reality. The fact is that there is a prior sense for the real which pervades and tests all language and all stories.

The clue to the relation between story-worlds and real world is to be found in that motif of "interest" on which I have laid such stress. In all those features of storying which exert their spell on hearer or reader we can recognize the bridge between fiction and life itself. Stories would not even exist or be heard through if human nature did not look to them avidly for illumination of its homelessness in time and circumstance. It is just because life is a labyrinth that we follow eagerly the clues and traces, the impasses and detours and open sesames of a myth or tale. The world of a story is our own world in a higher register.

V

But it is not enough thus to vindicate the importance of story-world. It is equally required that we take account of the vast differences in stories. Here it is not just a question of different *genres* (folktales, fairy tales, legends, parables, allegories, etc.), different *theaters of action* (ancient or modern, East or West, hut or palace, war or peace, etc.), different *plot-lines* (comedy, tragedy), different *thematics* (didactic, heroic, hagiographic, etc.). All such scenarios of "what happened" appeal, indeed, to a deeply rooted interest in the structure of circumstance and the web of becoming. Apart from such differences many

4. (London: Faber & Faber, 1959).

of these dramatic actions are circumscribed in one way or another. Thus social myths like those of Horatio Alger or Paul Bunyan or Faust or Prometheus are determined by this or that particular cultural horizon. Many vivid rehearsals transcribe persuasively this or that vicissitude but there is a great difference in what is included and what is left out. So we are led to ask not only Is that a true story? but Is that the whole story?

In evaluating stories no doubt we should take account of expert literary criteria, as for example in the case of novels. The best critics have their schooled perceptions for discriminating the rhetorics and quality of a tale. But they work in their own bailiwick and recognize that more ultimate soundings are "not in their brief." Our task, furthermore, is a difficult one because we should look deeper than what may be recognized as the universal popular appeal of a story. Such sway over the imagination of multitudes or even epochs is certainly a testimony to its importance, but we still ask as to its horizon and assumptions.

To appraise narratives in this searching way will no doubt trouble those who would leave the bard or romancer fancy-free. If, indeed, one can look for some kind of truth to life in a story yet one should not expect to find it in the same way or measure in every story. Even the most gratuitous fabling is to be honored and may tell us something about ourselves. Granted, however, that we should recognize the rights of invention and the free play of imagination there still remains the task of discrimination.

I have suggested that some kind of truth to life should be expected, but we should go deeper than this. What we take to be true to life may be very shallow and distorted. We may like a story or a history just because it is true to life as *we* see it, but that story or history may be far from telling the whole story. A story may be all the better precisely because it is *not* true to life as commonly recognized. Even if it be true to what we may see as a deeper view of life, that view also may be conventional and that truth very partial. It is at this point that the structural critics have put us on our guard. The worlds we take for granted differ a great deal, and we have all been brainwashed in different ways.

How can we evaluate stories in this situation? I would say that it is in terms of how far they clarify just these uncertainties. Many narratives merely play on our inbuilt expectations and flatter our habitual dreams. Without being moralistic we shall value stories which challenge these mental habits, take in more dimensions of our human experience, and so orient us more searchingly in the real givens of life.

In weighing narratives we should look, therefore, to what I would call the *urgency* of the fabulation. This takes us back to the basic question: Why were stories told in the first place? Like language itself the prompting to story was pragmatic, a matter of fateful orientation and survival. At any stage we can ask what motivates the discourse and the telling. How rooted and urgent is the impulse to world-making? To what parameters of our human nature is the storying responsive?

There are great differences in the vigor and grasp which prompt the myth-maker and teller-of-tales, and consequently in the scope of reality with which they wrestle and which they report. Looking at the matter culturally we can recognize periods, as we have seen, in which any impulse to evoke the past in recital was undeveloped. The sense of time and continuity, and of moral agency in them, was unawakened.

But so in our later eras there will be more or less robustness in the urge to storying. Where it is anemic, narrative will bear the marks of the oneiric, the dreamlike. The story-line will be directed by wish and wish fulfillment, by syndromes and dramas of the psyche, rather than by engagement with the actual.

Story-worlds, thus, are shaped by more or less articulated grasp of our human actuality. Their range runs from involuntary dreaming—all that we call fantasy and escape—by way of such wonderful fabling as we find in the Buddhist *Journey to the West* in course of translation by Anthony Yu,[5] in which a phantasmagoria of myth and dream is interwoven with humor and instruction, to fictions long or short in which the scenarios reflect and reorganize lived experience and mapped wisdom. These last, whether epics or novels or tales, often do, indeed, transcribe urgent wrestling with multilevel aspects of our

---

5. (Chicago: University of Chicago Press, vol. 1, 1977; vol. 2, 1978).

human experience though in partial and incomplete ways. Here we must continue to ask whether they tell the whole story.[6]

But we should also be prepared to recognize that some stories are not true stories, not just because they do not tell the whole story but because their original motivation is vitiated. As in dreams or paranoia the scenario may be governed by deep-seated factors which make for illusion. We need only think of the way in which the most commonplace anecdote in gossip may be distorted by malice, or the way in which a lust for destruction may prompt sensationalism in a film. Many popular as well as more pretentious novels are fraudulent—and this is to be distinguished from immoral—because writer and reader conspire to dream a world in accordance with their own wishes, or resentments. Many readers are deceived by such romances or inventions since they gloss over what is difficult.

With respect to all stories the question therefore is to be pressed as to how searching is the exploration of "happening." There are various kinds of traps which the true storyteller must overcome. Language has its inertia; narration has its constraining patterns and runs in habituated channels; the imagination has its seductions and the heart has its idols. The narrator who would tell the whole story in some given account must dominate these obstacles. So too the

6. Two well-known narratives may be briefly noted to illustrate my criteria. Jorge Luis Borges's "The Gospel According to Mark" is a masterly tour de force. What motivated the story is the challenge to provide a literary transcription of the power of myth. So Borges narrates the enactment of a world-old drama, that of the ritual execution of the tribal king. But in conflating the sacrifice with that of the Christ story we cannot but have a sense of artifice. A more plausible portrayal of the fanaticism and sadomasochism in question lies beyond the frame of the fiction. As in a problem in chess the author is first of all motivated to explore a literary analogue for the myth, but his success at this level is bought at the price of any deeper probe.

William Faulkner's *Light in August* is vulnerable at a different point. Here we can recognize how deeply motivated storying may be not so much truncated as diverted. This novel like some others of the author exhibits the way in which unconscious social syndromes can control the scenario: cultural nostalgias, or psychic dramas related to miscegenation. These "stories" with their hyperdramatic resonances (castration, etc.) assert themselves in conflict with the project of the author.

In both cases the telltale sensationalism is an index to the latent cleavage. Contrast *Anna Karenina* and Beckett's *All That Fall* in both of which such a potentially melodramatic climactic episode as death under the wheels of a train is so deeply contextualized as to be integral to the fable and unsensational.

listener/reader, though he enters willingly into the spell of a story, will especially prize those stories which *dispel* the sway of other story-worlds in which he has been held captive.

After all, as I have urged, behind our clouded visions of the world there is a prior sense for the real which continues to test them. The surpassing plenitude of existence haunts our groping dreams and fictions. Deeper than our illusions or even our better myths and fables is an original and constitutive link with creation itself. It is thanks to this primordial source or taproot in the real that we wrestle with phantom worlds, and it is here that imagination and language are empowered, as in our greatest stories, to transcribe not only the true texture of living but its transcendent horizons and promise.

10

Between Reminiscence and History

The life of the past is a dry leaf, crackled, without sap or chlorophyll, riddled with gaps, frayed with rents, which held up to the light, offers at most a skeletal net-work of its slender and brittle nerves. Special efforts are required to restore to it its fleshed-out and green aspect as a leaf in its prime, to recapture for events and incidents that plenitude which overwhelms the living and keeps them from imagining anything else.

Marguerite Yourçenar,
Souvenirs pieux

I propose to reflect with you on some aspects of informal reminiscence, impromptu recollection, and its relation to history proper. I am grateful to the Massachusetts Historical Society for its indulgence on this occasion of reminiscence rather than research, and of miscellany rather than monograph. As some kind of historian I share a certain shudder with you at this declension from proper archival propriety. I hasten to add, however, that my concern here is not first of all with any particular reminiscences of my own. Any such will be introduced only for purposes of illustration, though I shall be pleased if they awake any echoes among my older contemporaries.

What I have in mind as reminiscence runs from idle anecdotes in a bar or club, or news-mongering in a neighborhood, to more significant evocations of the past at a family reunion or among old soldiers or among any who have shared significant experiences. I have in

This chapter appeared originally in *The Proceedings of the Massachusetts Historical Society* 87 (1975). I wish to pay tribute here to then-director Stephen Reilly.—A.N.W.

view first of all oral recital. But of course it is not far from this kind of fragmentary rehearsal to such written record as goes into a private letter or journal.

What is interesting about all this is that we are at the roots of history and historiography. For better or worse we can see the past taking shape. What goes on in this kind of reportage interests me as a student of early Christianity because of the great importance in its study of the oral tradition and its forms, and of the role of anonymous eyewitnesses and reporters in the diffusion of the gospel. Going farther afield, I am also drawn to this topic by what is suggested in recent studies of recital and fabulation among folklorists and anthropologists. There is no great distance from popular reminiscence to folklore, saga and myth.

It seems to me that anyone interested in historiography can learn a good deal by watching what goes on in casual reminiscence. No doubt a great deal of extempore anecdotage and swapping of memories is gratuitous, fragmentary and uncontrolled. But what transpires here is a kind of paradigm of history writ large. Common to both is the same fundamental human impulse to keep the past alive, to establish continuities in experience, an impulse toward orientation. If we evoke the past for entertainment either formally or informally it is more than a question of amusement. Some sort of deep gratification is operative. We are finding ourselves, affirming ourselves, even defending ourselves.

Perhaps what we are here pointing to is the universal impulse toward saga. Every tribe and neighborhood and club builds up its saga, and such recital represents both entertainment and self-definition: it celebrates the past and orients the present. This is as true of formal history as of informal evocation.

I have spoken of the deep gratification that is operative in reminiscing. Passion and avidity go into it. When old comrades put their heads together in a chain of anecdotes no one can miss the excitement. It is hard to break up such a session. Only the outsider is bored. That is because he misses his own histories.[1]

---

1. A similar inside-outside situation is evoked by Wilmarth Lewis as between devotees of either Trollope or Jane Austen. "Like Austenians," he writes, "Trollopians can and do talk by the hour about the characters and incidents in their master's novels, a form of reminiscence that is asphyxiating to outsiders" (*One Man's Education* [New York, 1967], 221).

On one side the appetite for reminiscence is related to the impulse to gossip. The whole gamut of human emotion and attitude can be reflected in our choice and manner of storytelling: vanity, malice, lust, jealousy but also laughter, grief, admiration, affection and exuberance. Reminiscing like history proper has its deeper dynamics and compulsions. We are reminded of von Humboldt's view of language as "energy." The loquacity, vivacity, volubility of the human animal are the expressions of his psychic energy. We talk, talk, talk, we spread news, we tell stories, accumulate saga, write epics out of a profound compulsion. The Germans have a word for it, *Erzähler-freude.*

On its unhealthy side the deep seduction of invidious recital is exposed in the Book of Proverbs:

> The words of a whisperer are like delicious morsels;
> they go down into the inner parts of the body. (Prov. 18:8)

The prestige of anonymous talebearing is dramatized in a famous passage of Vergil dealing with Rumor. But these are only negative aspects of the whole phenomenon of reportage and news. Men and women have big ears for any story that concerns them. Thus our attention to even unimportant aspects of reminiscence has its justification. The cause of truth is difficult from the beginning, and the task of the historian is not only that of arbiter but also like that of a tamer of wild horses.

Another point at which attention to reminiscence may be illuminating has to do with its fragmentary character. When we tell stories about the past there are of course gaps and omissions. Interest is selective. The spotlight is not only on particular events, topics, persons. It is also a question of level or depth. When village annals are embroidered in a barbershop the anecdotes may be informative at a very superficial level. But we know occasions when among colleagues or intimates the richer implications of the past are sounded.

I must observe here in passing that to me the most searing examples of profound flashback in modern literature are the two short dramatic pieces of Samuel Beckett, *Krapp's Last Tape* and *Embers.* These no doubt represent a very private kind of recall, but they suggest the fatefulness and perhaps the exorcistic power of memory.

Even in shared reminiscence there is a great difference between the retailing of facts and an interpretive rehearsal; between differing degrees of plasticity in the telling. Life has its octaves and its diapasons. It may take a poet to convey the past in its thickness and its resonances.

But all this applies to formal history also. Here too we are prepared for lacunae, for distortion, for abstraction, for superficiality. Official history may properly wish to correct the vagaries of private recollection, but it may well learn something from its liveliness and plasticity. The historian rightly seeks to link up in a wider pattern the isolated testimonies of particular witnesses. But in so doing he may forfeit connection with the inwardness and vitality of the initial recitals, the grass-roots fabulation. One can cite here an analogy from the field of science. The specialist does not always have the advantage over the amateur. The habituated categories of the professional investigator may blind him. Sometimes naivete is aware of matters which escape expertise.

One can illustrate this aspect of the matter by the contribution of two poets to our repossession of the past with respect to the Civil War. Walt Whitman was on the scene and has left us his eyewitness documentation in prose and verse. Carl Sandburg was not on the scene, but as a later biographer of Lincoln he helps to safeguard similar dimensions of our national memory. I would suggest that today our contemporary poets can open up for us significant issues of our Bicentennial. I think of Archibald MacLeish, author of "America Was Promises." I think also of Robert Penn Warren, author of the long narrative poem about Jefferson's American dream, *Brother to Dragons*, and of Robert Lowell, author of the historical dramatic series, *The Old Glory*.

To return, however, to impromptu recollection and recital: here we have, as it were, history in its prenatal stage. Later public history is here in germ, in gestation. The lines are being drawn. The map of time is being adumbrated. Even if error is disseminated it is hard later to correct it. In any case later formal history is largely built on the testimony of eyewitnesses, whether as regards facts, interpretations, valuations, but especially as regards the whole thrust of recall and its horizons. The animating spirit of the local or national saga goes back to the initial impulse, motivations, vision.

I turn again to my own field of historiography to illustrate. We would not have any Gospels in the New Testament except for the first anonymous oral witnesses and storytellers. Their crucial role in the later strata of tradition is transparent in the frequent references to the reports about Jesus that were bruited abroad. This was impromptu recital and uncontrolled reportage. The rise of Christianity was inseparable from it. We hear of "fame," "rumor," "news." For example: "But so much the more went there a fame abroad of him" (Luke 5:15); "And his fame went through all Syria" (Matt. 4:24). Or later with respect to Paul's field of action: "From you sounded out the word of the Lord" (1 Thess. 1:5).

Now it is true that this initial grass-roots dissemination by eyewitnesses had to do with unique events. Its high seriousness may distinguish it from much casual anecdotage. But it calls our attention to what one may call the subsoil of any history-in-the-making. Even after the oral stage had been largely superseded by the writing stage in the new movement, this kind of viva voce testimony continued and lent immediacy and vitality to the tradition. Even after the Gospels were circulating we hear the Church Father Papias confessing that he preferred what he called "the living and abiding voice," that is, oral accounts by surviving witnesses where they could be heard. We all recall how Robert Browning exploited this theme with regard to the aged John, supposedly the last survivor of the apostles, in his poem "A Death in the Desert."

What must concern us all is how vulnerable the past is to loss and distortion. As the actuality of the present moment recedes from us it immediately begins to fade, to be forgotten, to be warped in meaning, to be disputed. The past is immediately problematic, in the small and in the large. The image of the past is at the mercy of every sort of vagary, accident, pressure, fashion. The past is a kind of no-man's-land arbitrarily charted, a *terra* with the larger part *incognita*. If this is true of a nation or civilization it is also true of local history. If it is true of the past of a city it is also true of your past and mine. If it is true of the first or thirteenth century it is also true of yesterday. To some extent Rilke's exclamation applies to all of us: "Est-il possible que tous ces gens connaissent parfaitement un passé qui n'a jamais existé!"[2]

---

2. *Les cahiers de Malte Laurids Brigge* (Paris, 1926), 30.

These observations only reinforce the responsibility of the historian and the fateful importance of his labors. He has the austere and surgical task of cutting through all such confusion and delusion, all the more difficult because it is not only a question of facts but of their interpretation. And since our past is inseparable from our present the historian like the psychiatrist and the confessor obliges the individual and the society to see themselves in the mirror of truth.

Much of the past gets lost and what is not lost gets distorted. A personal experience of my own reinforces this reflection on the hazards of reminiscence. On July Fourth, 1917, I was at the Picpus Cemetery in Paris near Lafayette's grave when the famous words, "Lafayette, we are here!" were spoken. Although I heard the address I used to say that our commander-in-chief, Pershing, had spoken the words. Indeed this was widely reported. As a matter of fact it is Colonel C.E. Stanton who should have the credit. If one looks at histories of World War I and accounts of Pershing's career, including his own *My Experience in the World War*,[3] one will find a great many contradictions in the way the episode is reported. Stanton is assigned differing ranks and offices. The chief address of the occasion is attributed by some to Stanton and elsewhere to Brand Whitlock. The French War Minister Painlevé insisted that Pershing say something himself. Pershing writes that he cannot recall what he said extempore. A French historian of World War I, however, Paul Delay, like Herodotus, supplies Pershing's exact words.[4]

The most colorful account is in Laurence Stalling's book, *The Doughboys*. After describing how Captain Stanton stepped forward and saluted and cried, "Nous voilà, Lafayette!" he continues, "The French brass, sticklers for military protocol, insisted that the commanding general say something. He could well have said, 'Où est le lavabo?' for all it mattered in the weeping, shouting, laughing maelstrom."[5]

What had led me to assign the famous phrase to Pershing fits in with an old observation about historical sources. Anecdotes tend to float and to attach themselves to prominent figures. There is a

---

3. Vol. 1 (New York, 1931), 93.
4. *La guerre hors de France: Les Etats-Unis* (Paris, 1920), 327–28.
5. (New York, 1963), 15.

dramatic impulse at work here which affects even our perception of an event not to mention our later reconstruction of it. If Pershing did not speak the words he should have.

As for the impulse to transfer tradition from the lesser to the greater figure, we have a remarkable example in Holy Writ. There is good reason to think that Mary's hymn of rejoicing, the Magnificat, in the first chapter of Luke was originally ascribed to her cousin Elizabeth, the mother of John the Baptist. There is strong textual evidence for this, and many scholars accept it. So Mary gets what was Elizabeth's as Pershing received what was Stanton's. In the words of one even greater, "To him that hath shall be given, and from him that hath not shall be taken away even that which he hath."

But this has only been a parenthesis, one example of the risks, lacunae, distortions in reminiscence. One could add further types of imperfect recollection. One could say that such corruption has its own laws, as in the case of copyists' errors. In remembering we tend to skip or displace. We conflate originally distinct events. We tend to dramatize, exaggerate, moralize. The artistic and rhetorical impulse is at work at even a preliterary level. Even a person who keeps a journal is unconsciously guided by a genre model, just as the private letter is shaped by an epistolary convention. These models and conventions dictate style, selection, omission. The genre sets the focus. The medium orients the matter. So with oral recital.

There are other features of reminiscence that can be noted, and these also bear upon more formal narrative. Anecdotes, as we have suggested, tend to gather about well-known persons or families— both in the village and the metropolis. Furthermore, they specially favor unusual happenings, contrasts, ironies, paradoxes and of course the marvelous.

Their range is determined by the circle in question. Different groups share different pasts and each reverts to its own heroes, villains and topics. The repertoire will vary with the company. This makes difficulty for the historian who would like to eavesdrop on all. Thus one will hear differing types of anecdotes and differing aspects of the past according to whether the situation is that of a high table at an Oxford College or an English pub; whether one is in a leather chair at the Century Club or at a Hibernian picnic or in a State House cloakroom. In each case the *topoi* will differ.

In some situations politics or religion or sex will be tabu. In each case narrative style, tone, tenor and vocabulary will be, as it were, predetermined.

I have been speaking of reminiscence that intends to be responsible. Of course the risks of reportage have to allow for deliberate falsification. The figure of the boaster is familiar in literature and in life. In Eugene O'Neill's play, *A Touch of the Poet*, we have an example of a veteran who so fabricated a heroic past for himself that he could not survive its exposure. Other memorialists shape the past to vindicate a party or a cause, and in such a way that the line between good faith and fraud is hard to draw.

What I have been observing has again an interesting relation to the familiar category of gossip, if I may return to this topic. One could say that the gamut of informal recital runs from gossip at the lower end of the scale to authentic eyewitness at the other. Even in other kinds of historical sources such as private letters we have elements of gossip. And gossip has an importance of its own in shaping the image of life and the past. Anyone who has lived in a village can corroborate this. Gossip is one of the handmaids of Clio. If gossip is notoriously fallible yet it is an index of outlook and opinion in a group. It corresponds in a wider sphere to the myths of a nation, or the stories that a people tells itself.

If it is important for a later historian to know what really happened at a given time, it is also important for him to know what a people at the time *thought* had happened and *how* they thought about it. With all their errors and delusions and even slanders, gossip and hearsay shape the public image of history. What happens here in the village or neighborhood has its analogy in the wider society, for here too there is an underground of fables, clichés, consensus, axioms in which truth and falsehood are mixed, and which is very resistant to historical correction.

Gossip is usually colorful and emotive; valuations and attitudes betray themselves. Anecdotes and characterizations are marked by playfulness, satire, admiration, innuendo, spite, etc. What the historian calls tendentiousness in more formal reporting is already manifest. But all of this is truly documentary and revelatory in another sense. The novelist knows the importance of gossip. Think of the considerable part it plays in Joyce's *Ulysses* and *Finnegan's Wake*.

Gossip like other forms of spontaneous recital, for better or worse, begins to set the lines in which history is remembered.

It is only a step from oral reminiscence to the kind of immediate recording represented by a private diary or a personal letter. It is true that journals and letters usually recount circumstances of the moment rather than memories proper. But here too we recognize the informality, the spontaneity, of the reportage. Here too we have a kind of grass-roots witness to the passage of time. In both cases we are only at the vestibule of formal history. History has not yet gone public. Compare for example a personal account, either oral or in a letter, to a newspaper report of the same happenings. The one is eyewitness, the other is commonly secondhand. But this is only an initial stage of what happens when one passes from private narration to public and official chronicle.

These considerations, of course, bear directly upon such historical repositories as that represented by this society. Special importance in our archives attaches to what we might call the prehistorical survivals made up of letters, journals, handbills, a sea captain's logbook, a general's orderly book.[6] These are ephemera and just for that reason irreplaceable. Even their physical form is revelatory. These were "for the moment," and therefore authentic. These were jottings and scribblings, not literature. These were unconscious reflexes—in Wallace Stevens's phrase, "the cry of its occasion"—and therefore uniquely documentary. But this same character attaches to casual reminiscence.

It is again not a great step from a private journal to published autobiography. An autobiography is an extended reminiscence and is rather material for history than history proper. In such memoirs one can identify the same impulses and motivations that preside over oral reminiscence. But instead of viva voce exchange oriented to the immediate hearers and their common pool of experience—the

6. General Artemas Ward's Orderly Book detailing his orders and dispositions during the Siege of Boston, in the possession of this society, is one example of such bare bones of history. Any later expansion of the course of events must flesh it out but can hardly depart from it. The official War Office history of World War I includes in its many volumes a corresponding austere serial listing of day-by-day and hour-by-hour orders affecting the division and brigade and regiment in which I served in France in 1917–18. It is a strange experience today to read these laconic orders from above which determined the scenario of the lives and deaths of our hosts.

special acoustics of oral recital—an autobiography is written at a
desk for an invisible and postponed audience of readers. The same
thing happens as when the Homeric oral cycle was frozen by writing,
as Parry and Lord describe it. Impromptu vivacity and immediate
resonance are forfeited in favor of an enduring record.

In autobiography one is on the way from reminiscence to history.
But here too one is struck by the differing levels at which the past is
evoked in anecdote and portrayal. This has come home to me in
reading comparatively recent autobiographies in which my own
experience overlapped with that of the authors, those of Wilmarth
Lewis and Edward Weeks. With Lewis I shared school days at
the Thacher School as well as college scenes and other associations.
Like Weeks I was in the American Field Service in World War I.
I followed therefore with special attention their versions of similar
annals, their selection, their emphasis, their tone and special optic.

To illustrate in the case of Wilmarth Lewis's memoir, *One Man's
Education*:[7] Lewis recognizes that the past, like a musical score, has
not only its various themes and motifs, but also its octaves, voices,
overtones and undertones. He restores to the faded annals in
Marguerite Yourçenar's phrase "that plenitude which overwhelms
the living." His combination of quick sensibility and wide curiosities,
acting like a photographic developer, brings to light a wide gamut of
life's transactions. We have a test here of any kind of recital, including that of formal history.

Edward Weeks's engaging memoir, *My Green Years*,[8] reminds us
of what a large part Boston, Harvard and New England had in the
origin and accomplishments of the American Field Service in World
War I before this country entered the conflict. Weeks tells us that
when he went to France in 1917 his uniform had sewn into it a
portion of a tricolor sash which had once belonged to Lafayette. The
latter had taken it off to drape Weeks's great-grandmother at a
welcoming ceremony at Castle Garden in New York in 1824. She
had delivered an address of greeting to him in French at the age of
thirteen.

Beyond the official histories of the Field Service and of the Lafayette Escadrille someone could well examine today the antecedents in

7. New York, 1967.
8. Boston, 1973.

this region and elsewhere of the feeling for France which was so large a part of the motivation. Let me reminisce and testify that it was more than a matter of superficial sentiment and rhetoric. Even more than in the case of England, the mother country, it was a matter of the meaning of Western civility. It had to do with the Latin and Roman underpinnings of our sense of the *res publica*, the republic. Thomas Jefferson, especially in his architectural preferences, testifies to this tradition.

At a reunion of World War I and II Field Service volunteers some years ago, George Van Santvoord, former head of the Hotchkiss School, gave a moving tribute to the French common soldiers as we knew them: extenuated but enduring after three years of trench warfare, exceeded but with a childlike vivacity and talent for the impossible. On one occasion I stopped my model-T Ford ambulance by the road where several French soldiers were having their noonday meal. They welcomed me into their animated argot talk and sliced off for me portions of their army bread and sausage. The American latecomer in his smart whipcord uniform from Lloyd's felt that he was initiated into a faded horizon-blue fraternity which stretched from the Jura and the Vosges to Verdun and the Somme, into a solidarity that extended back three years, and even further to the times of Napoleon and Joan of Arc. History should have a place for these kinds of nuances and diapasons.

I close with one further speculation about reminiscence. As I have said we take pleasure in such rehearsals not only as a matter of entertainment. We are moved by an impulse to hold on to the past but also to map it and establish continuities with it. We push back the encircling oblivion and expand the Now. But it is also a matter of orientation, our place in a scheme of things. As we share in an anecdote or historical evocation our sense of reality is enhanced. This is as true of a vignette of family recollection as of our national saga.

Modern study of the folktale and of epic has illuminated these aspects of recital. One can go even farther with the social anthropologists: a tribal tradition is therapeutic. Its narrative can have the character of what is called "performative" language, as in a ritual of exorcism. Rehearsal of the tribal memory and myth restores and illumines. And something like this prompts our own best retrospect and historiography.

11

Post-Modern Reality and the Problem of Meaning

Méfiez-vous de l'abyssal autant que du céleste.

—Henri Lefebvre.
(A now faded legend on the walls of the
Faculté des Lettres at Nanterre.)

How far is it true that cumulative modern factors have eroded our traditional categories and contexts of meaning? In what respects, for example, have the logical axioms and symbolic repertoire of the Academy been placed in question? Is the Western world, indeed, passing through a mutation such that we must disallow our ancient humanistic quest for reality in favor of some supposed anterior order of apprehension?

I

The wider question here is that of the inevitable conditioning of language and meaning by cultural change. My special interest in the present analysis is in those shifts in the modern outlook and sensibility in the West which have occasioned not only changes in the arts and all cultural expressions but also problems with respect to the legacies of the past. It is to be recognized that these momentous changes have involved not only ideas, values, taste and life-style but

This chapter was written as a contribution to a volume honoring Paul Ricoeur. The project could not be completed, and some of the contributions, including this one, were published in the journal *Man and World* 13 (1980).—A.N.W.

also basic apperception and our sense of reality. There is no question that this situation raises basic questions as to orientation in the present, continuity with the past and projections into the future.

I shall give more particular attention farther on to the term "post-modern" and the ways in which it is used and the issues it raises. Even where the term itself is not employed recent discussion of the outcomes of "modernism" and "avant-garde" by such writers as Octavio Paz, George Steiner, R. Poggioli and Frank Kermode suggests a radical break or dilemma in Western culture with respect to which various interpretations, various options, are open. It is with the more hyperbolic interpretations of this kairos and apocalyptic options that I am here chiefly concerned. The situation, the reality-problem, of the age is rightly to be recognized and explored. But those solutions which revoke the past and seek another reality by this or that explosion of language or in some occult dynamics of the self—these various versions of a new gnosticism, versions acclaimed by many who appeal expressly to the post-modern, these I am concerned to challenge.

Fate and the human condition are not so easily escaped. Culture with all its detritus and tyrannies has to be wrestled with, not shed off. Humanism, rationality and their forum, the university, however subject to reform and enrichment, continue. Language with its freight, like our genes and chromosomes, persists through flood and apocalypse.

Assessment of our situation can indeed vary. At this point I shall only call attention to a few general observations. Before we reach too radical a conclusion as to the discontinuity of our moment we may well reflect on our lack of distance and on the myopia of the Zeitgeist. Periodization, the delimiting of epochs, is safest in long retrospect. History is not wanting in examples of those who thought that they lived at closing time. A certain kind of seduction operates which leads those involved in novel stresses or euphorias to assign even cosmic overtones to their local engagement. Even apart from apocalyptic forecasts one can see the impulse at work in Hegel or in Jonathan Edwards who in his *The Plan of Redemption* saw the world-story reaching its denouement in his own day.

Another consideration is the pluralism of our cultural traditions. They do not all evolve in the same direction. Erosion of older stabilities proceeds at a slower pace in some sectors of society. Those intellectual circles most acutely aware of a changing sensibility may register accurately the alienation at work in wide strata, but may be out of touch with the wider public. The deeper unpredictables of history often take our elites by surprise, and the deracinated school-man or Bohemian is a poor judge of hidden root systems and their fertility.

A major consideration of this general kind has to do with our sense of the past. Surely any judicious appraisal of our modern crisis depends in part on an adequate and living sense of our historical antecedents. Orientation in time like orientation in space requires far-reaching perspectives and triangulation. This means more than formal acquaintance with classics or the latest knowledge as to the chronology of early man. It means a mimetic identification with the human story, and an imaginative rehearsal and moral vision of its ordeals, miscarriages and survivals.

Without minimizing the jeopardies and bestialities of our own epoch, these should at least be envisaged against the background of the chaotic upheavals and devastations of the past. Our own radical disorder however unprecedented has its continuities with that past and with the human lot, and fixation on it in isolation from that wider present which includes the past can only mean a lapse into unreality.

But this tyranny of the contemporary, even in its less hyperbolic forms, also obscures and disallows the legacies of the past. No doubt our better culture-critics know their history and its monuments. But their long and understandable preoccupation with the modern epoch in its aspect of iconoclasm tends to subvert such depth of perspective. Those very curiosities and emancipations which define them as "modern" act as a mask to shut out a more total humanism. In younger adepts, often less profoundly initiated, this unbalance often takes on the features of an ideology. For all intents and purposes the world began in the seventeenth century or at some later point. Thus today the term "mutation" can be all too loosely invoked.

I can illustrate the matter in terms of the more recent past. In connection with the American Bicentennial and in justified revulsion against shallow and chauvinist sentiment associated with its rituals, one could hear hyperbolic arraignments of the Republic and apoca-lyptic verdicts on the American Dream. These came often from shrill voices of the counterculture who were evidently judging in terms of their own short life spans which did not go back to World War II. The world began for many such with Vietnam. In the announced topic for one such discussion an inspired typesetter substituted the word "apoplectic" for "apocalyptic": "Apoplectic Dimensions of America's Manifest Destiny."

All such reverse Pollyannaism which would paint our people in such dark colors and assimilate our imminent fall to that of Babylon and Tyre traces again to a foreshortened perspective. Reactions of outrage and scandal arising out of our recent sorry history are fully in order. But why such shocked surprise! One could ask the wider question as to how much real knowledge of real evil is still transmitted among our more emancipated youth. But this is only a smaller paradigm for the wider culture shock of those who read the impasse of our age in post-modern terms with all its implications of panic, liberation and fantasy.

One can agree with those who recognize an epochal change in our period—yet hardly of that order of which David Jones spoke when he said that "the world turned," referring to man's discovery of fire and to the crucifixion of Christ. Granted the change there can be different ways of construing it. There are epochs and epochs. Some can see a cycle and some a spiral. Some can see a terminus and some a milestone. Some can see a lapse into chaos and some a renewal. Some can see a law of recurrence and some, entropy.

To identify our cultural moment as post-modern, or more generally to see the long Western erosion of older authorities as having reached a stage of dissolution—this kind of appraisal suggests many kinds of reflection, not least for the theologian. Interpretation of the times is a main theme in the biblical tradition, going back especially to the great world-assize in the forty-first chapter of Isaiah. Here the coastlands and the ends of the earth are summoned together with Israel, and all are challenged to give a reading of the enigmas of the age, of what is afoot in the divine counsels. The hearing is opened, the idols are challenged. They remain silent and the tableau ends in derision.

> Set forth your case, says the Lord . . .
> Tell us the former things, what they are
>   that we may consider them,
> that we may know their outcome;

or declare to us the things to come.
Tell us what is to come hereafter,
    that we may know that you are gods . . .
[Silence; no answer]
Behold, you are nothing
    and your work is naught.

Thus the author, whom we call Second Isaiah, rebukes the ignorance of the Babylonian oracles in their appraisal of the trends of history but also that of the Hebrew exiles. Looking beneath the shows and enigmas of the years he sees reversal where the idols see continuity and a "new thing" where the exiles see only anomie. But that new thing represents a deeper continuity beneath the anomie, continuity with the ancient pattern of the Exodus.

II

Telling the time, discernment of ends and beginnings, has had a long history both in Christian theology and in Western humanism, and other cultures have had their counterparts. It has often been observed that eschatologies and Utopias mirror the values of their authors or societies. The same will be true of our own modern periodizations. The revolutions of the times are calibrated by us in terms of our own investments.

To see our historical moment as one marking the end of the age of humanism, both biblical and Hellenic, can, as in the case of Nietzsche's death of God, be both liberating and terrifying. But these kinds of absolutes and antinomianisms have a seductive appeal which should warn us. The burden of history cannot so easily be put off. Scenarios of evasion into total liberty in images of the sea and its limitlessness, and of the freebooter and pirate, have recurred in French poetry from the time of Rimbaud. "To the depths of the unknown to find the new," wrote Baudelaire. These impulses also surfaced in the fantasy life of the students in the riots in Paris in the late sixties.

Even less radical revulsions against the human past may be motivated by similar persuasions of innocence and autonomy. It is particularly in its critique of the Academy that extreme views of our modern crisis can be scrutinized. If an old brainwashed saeculum of law and intimidation has come to an end and we are in a post-Christian and post-modern situation, if not only bourgeois mentality but an epoch of rationality, objectivity and ego-consciousness is passing into one of prepersonal *eros* or some alternative reality, then one can understand the widespread disaffection with regard to the schools and learning. If Hebrew *DBR*, Greek *nous*, Latin *ratio* and Christian *logos* are to be disavowed in favor of some new occult register of meaning, some deeper somatic or affectional *episteme*,[1] where is the court which will adjudicate our explorations? What the critics of academia above all crave is some shortcut to gnosis, thus shunning the ongoing forum of discrimination with its burden, its involvement and its responsibility to the whole of human experience with its diverse transcriptions old and new.

Because of the radical break with Western humanism represented by the post-modern stance I find it appropriate to mention here that my first contact with Paul Ricoeur was at the 500th Anniversary Festival of the University of Basel in June 1960, on which occasion an honorary doctorate was conferred upon him. The cultural history of the West evoked in the academic, ecclesiastical and civic ceremonies of that occasion throws into sharp relief the values and vicissitudes of that tradition which is widely threatened today. The University was founded by Pius II, Aeneas Sylvius Piccolomini, lover of learning, and its earliest teachers included such associates and contemporaries of Erasmus and Reuchlin as Sebastian Brant, Sebastian Castellio and Oecolampadius. Later figures in the various faculties are memorable, for example in biblical studies, Wettstein and de Wette. More recently we encounter such names as Jacob Burckhardt, Dilthey and Overbeck.

Even such a momentary focus upon one institution should arrest sweeping disparagement of centuries of labor in the arts and sciences. Whatever ruptures in the fabric of life may concentrate our attention or our passions today, we should not overlook the deeper web of civility and ethos nourished by such a paideia which continues in both public and clandestine ways in our own later societies.

---

1. A no doubt tongue-in-cheek paradigm of the alternatives by Celia Morris appeared in a circular of the Society for Values in Higher Education:
Our reading list's rather oppressive:
Buber and Tillich and such:
And sometimes we do not quite get them
So we think we will do feely-touch.

Polemic and ideological indictments of such antecedents do not take account of complexities and particulars. Many of our own priorities today have not been without their witness. I found one item in this history eloquent. Among the students who flocked to Basel from France, Italy, Germany, England, Hungary and Poland there was one immatriculated in 1585 named Didacus Lainus Americus Indus, in all probability an American Indian, who "being poor" was admitted without obligation of paying registration fees ("pauper, nichil"). "Perhaps he was attached to some printer as a corrector, since Basel printers were interested in the history of the Indian."[2]

One other consideration arises from this retrospect. Also in the roster of the Basel professors one finds the names of Paracelsus and Nietzsche. Though the former had only one embattled year of residence in the Faculty of Medicine, such names remind us that our humanist tradition and the academy have always had their rebels and prophets, and that in the long view an essential clearinghouse for the debate of cultural issues is within the university and not outside it or against it.

That the curricula of the fifteenth-century university could embrace wide poles is seen in the options offered between studies in the *via antiqua* (realism) and those in the *via moderna* (nominalism). In those days the latter position no doubt appeared as anarchic as some of the more iconoclastic frontiers of investigation and method appear today. But we owe our richer heritage in the following centuries to the fact that such cleavages were wrestled with in the corporations of learning—with their older antecedents in the medieval and classical schools—and that only those occultisms and gnosticisms were excluded or excluded themselves which refused the common grammar of reason. This hospitality to fatefully divergent outlooks goes back, indeed, to the medieval university, in which, as Lynn White has recently noted,[3] the opposition of the trivium to the quadrivium anticipated all later polarities between the humanities and the sciences. Yet such basic issues of epistemology and hermeneutic were confronted together under the common canopy of learning.

2. Reported in a study of the published registers of the University by Astrik L. Gabriel, in *Speculum: A Journal of Mediaeval Studies* 35 (July 1960): 498.
3. "Science and the Sense of Self: The Medieval Background of a Modern Confrontation," *Daedalus* (Spring 1978): 13–14, 59 (vol. 10.2 of The Proceedings of the American Academy of Arts and Sciences).

That the Academy of our day is open to the experience and shocks which have occasioned the revulsions, panics and fantasies of the post-modern mood was testified at Basel by the major public addresses delivered by Karl Jaspers and Adolf Portmann, the distinguished zoologist.[4]

With his topic, "Natural Science and Humanism," Portmann dealt with the promise and risk of our situation in the long perspective which is that of the biologist. Inevitably issues bearing on moral choice came to the fore, and therefore the humanist tradition of the West, not least because evolutionary variation is today open to conscious direction or manipulation. In this connection the speaker made some observations which bear directly on our topic: supposed cultural mutation as associated with the idea of post-modern discontinuity or novelty. The lesson from biology here is that fertile variation, healthy mutants as against "monsters" and abortions, depends upon millennially inbuilt codes in the germ or plasma which both limit and enrich new adaptations or species.

Recognizing that the essential factors in human mutation are no longer genetic but social-historical and noetic, this insight can be carried over to human cultural change. Here too continuity, in this case with ancient survival factors in the species, powers of adaptation and assimilation, is a condition of significant novelty. The dimension of freedom in our being may not arbitrarily disregard those long-established constants which, granted their variety in different societies, ensure our world-relatedness as well as our openness to existence. Inherited givens and codes may be creatively transformed but not abolished. To apply this to our present options, antinomian revulsion against the past and commitment to gratuity and the *novum* forfeit the ground of meaning and any purchase on reality.

In this area in an age like ours no doubt many discriminations, whether aesthetic or spiritual, remain open. But wisdom about these fateful borderlands between nature and history, givens and mutants, between ancient orders and innovation—discriminations which are both scientific and moral—can only be adequately canvassed in the

---

4. The addresses were published in *Die Fünfhundertjahrfeier der Universität Basel: Festhericht,* ed. Paul Roth (Basel: Birkhäuser Verlag, 1960), Jaspers' address, 60–77; Portmann's, 77–93.

university. Where else will even those who disparage the Academy look for qualified friends-in-court in the concern for *eros* and for true liberation?

Karl Jaspers in his address on "Truth and Science" reviewed the changes over five hundred years in the role of the university. Again its indispensable contribution as a communication center for the disparate traditions and cultural values of the modern world was emphasized.

> A wonderful quiet is granted to the university, safeguarded by the state. Scientific research, technical contribution, memory of the past and a shaping appropriation of its legacies—all this is admirable but insufficient. For the calm that is afforded the university is to the end that we should experience the storm of the course of the world in our hearts and minds, so as to grasp it. The university should be the site of the clearest consciousness of the age, where even that which is most alien is brought to the light—so that at this one point at least what is going on may be fully recognized, and that illumination diffusing itself in the world may be rich in benefits.

Jaspers ended his address with reflections on the atomic peril of our time and on the existential-moral demand thus imposed on all.

I have recalled this academic festival as one exhibit of a long and significant past, reaching down to our own day. If we understand it to be our task at a still later juncture to "name the real," we can ill afford to derogate the vicissitudes of man's commerce with the mysteries and his penultimate findings in periods still intimately linked with our own.

III

In any case in some modern or post-modern exploration the issue of "meaning" has been radically re-posed, and one can observe how incompatible such new orientation is with traditional academic axioms. I can illustrate by contemporary discussion of the novel. Here, inevitably, questions of realism, reference, objectivity, correspondence, meaning and meaningfulness arise. Our contemporary cultural disarray appears to have reached such an impasse in some quarters that the link between fabulation and actuality is broken. Of course if congruence with some supposed actuality or reality is thus dismissed one can still assign "meaning," without claims of representation, to ciphers and configurations of consciousness, viewed as indices of a nonself or "other" reality.

In a recent discussion of the modern novel by Bertrand Poirot-Delpeche[5] we are reminded that Balzac saw fiction as at least seeking to "rival reality." Since then with the loss of confidence in any such objective real to be transcribed or mirrored we have two schools which hold out for the survival of this genre. For one of these the Protean variability of the novel is so open that the sheer language strategies and incandescence of the writer will compensate for the loss of any kind of authorial reporting. At most his own epiphanic responses to the incommunicable are shared. The other school goes farther.

> It is no longer a question of reflecting one's own time with the help of a literary instrument supposedly trustworthy, but to explode that instrument so as to disclose whatever the language may conceal . . . of the unconscious—individual or collective—of death, or of absence.

In either case, the "death of the author" as traditionally understood, and the renunciation of an objective, accustomed "world" and its mimesis, highlights the sensibility of the post-modern as it is diagnosed by many.

Not only the novel as a form but narrativity itself comes under question in this context. This ancient mode of lending coherence to experience either by fiction or chronicle, either by myth or history, loses credibility when the reality of the world is decomposed. It is not surprising that the fictional plottings and scenarios of the last two centuries should be held suspect, conditioned as they have allegedly been by bourgeois perspectives. Even going farther back, when one of Samuel Beckett's characters (Henry in *Embers*) repudiates "stories, stories, years of stories" in his plea for a "voice," for a voice "now," Hugh Kenner notes of these "stories": "That is where the Newtonian universe belongs also: it was a story Europe told itself for many decades."[6]

But the challenge to narrative goes much farther than this. What is finally in question is that whole human *gestalt*, that ancient teleo-

---

5. "Mort de l'auteur," *Le Monde*, 27 janvier, 1978.
6. *Samuel Beckett* (New York, 1961), 184.

logical mentality, which finds orientation in "beginning, middle and end," in sequence and sequel, and in "the sense of an ending." Evidently this kind of critique strikes at all narrativity if not all fabulation. We see here a revulsion against rooted mental habits, a demand for the *novum*, which would turn from story to epiphany, from anecdote to happening, from statement to exclamation, from the plot to the aleatory. Evidences of this impulse are found not only in the mutations of the novel but at a more elementary level in a struggle with communication and with syntax itself, as in Beckett's fiction. Analogous quests are to be found in all the arts and their theory. Beyond the cultural stereotypes of plot, character, incident, setting with their all-too-familiar "meaning" we are to find "reality" in deeper enigmas and illuminations. Even the myths of the primitives are to be resolved into ultimate prelogical binaries.

We should have no quarrel with all such post-modern thrusts, aesthetic or critical, provided they are viewed as exploration rather than dogma. The issues raised are altogether worthy of debate, granted that some modalities of discursive exchange are acknowledged. But it is at this point that the competence of the humanist tradition is challenged. Yet what is important in the so-called post-modern sensibility can best be understood in the light of that tradition and its categories and logics. We have to do with continuity not discontinuity. But some of the motivations and projects of the more radical impulses of our period have been misconceived. There is such a thing as a rage for chaos as well as a rage for order.

The best tests of a tradition are often, indeed, the most radically adverse. It is only the most drastic shock or heightened tension which establishes the strength of a metal. So today our perilous Western phase of disarray and its apocalyptic or irrational or nihilist options will better bring to light and into fuller operation the human and humanist resources which have so long been under attack.

If my plea here against some forms of extreme iconoclasm represents a defense of tradition it should be clear that I welcome challenges to our heritage as it is understood either in our society or in the Academy. That I can sympathize with extreme contemporary voices should be clear from my comment on a disparagement of Samuel Beckett and his alleged program of "demolition" by André Marissel.

But I would urge that Beckett's program of demolition can still be seen as an ultimate effort to remove all masks as one aspect of a necessary lucidity at the point where he stands. In the right hands the iconoclasm of the antinovel and the drama of the absurd constitute an exploration of meaning. Since after all the artist in question continues to write rather than fall silent, the wrestle with language is not abandoned. But such an example highlights the language crisis of today in many quarters.[7]

And again, speaking of Beckett's struggle with solipsism and his "games" with numbers and series:

This is more than a "dry mock" of rationality. Nor should we say that in such contexts Beckett is a sheer nihilist. From within our confusion of tongues, from within our paralysis of authentic speech, he explores the gulf between the impersonal in our life and the human voice. That he pushes the dilemma to the utmost limit, the point of *stenachoria,* to use a Greek term—the anguishing impasse—and in mordant style, all this is only the artist's right to present a matter in its most illuminating exposure.[8]

It would seem clear to me that such responsible texts as those of Beckett and such issues as to meaning and meaninglessness, such issues of interpretation of the age or hermeneutic of consciousness, can be dealt with in the light of that very heritage which Beckett like others is concerned to explore. The dividing line between the real and the unreal, meaning and mania, must ultimately be determined by some link with human health and survival, some fiber or filament in consciousness which relates us to the order and plenitude of being. Our grasp of this as Occidentals is inevitably mediated to us through many confusions by our tradition.

For those who would claim or welcome a break with the tradition two cautionary observations are in order. One I have already suggested. Simple solutions, total revolt, apocalyptic reading of a situation always have their fascination. The lure of the absolute may also be compounded with hidden *ressentiment.* But another consideration should be weighed. Captivation with unknown possibilities is commonly dominated by the negative. The force of an antitraditional stance is often deceptive, like an echo. It borrows plausibility and

---

7. *The New Voice* (New York, 1969), 155.
8. Ibid., 148–49.

status from that which it opposes. Especially when hyperbolic repudiation and reversal are in question, as with blasphemy and scandal, their appeal is often parasitic on, and thus a tribute to, the tradition.

IV

I can throw into relief certain issues bearing on modernism and postmodernism by noting a few readings of our situation that warrant attention. The examples are taken from writers first of all concerned with literature and the arts rather than with philosophy or social science.

Certainly one of the most impressive probings of the turn of the times is to be found in the writings of Octavio Paz, and I have in mind his *Conjunctions and Disjunctions* (1969) and his *Children of the Mire: Modern Poetry from Romanticism to the Avant-Garde* (1974). We find here many of the motifs which come to the fore in sophisticated circles intent on a psychic and imaginative liberation and access to new spiritualities. Paz sees the whole movement reaching back to the end of the medieval world as an impulse of iconoclasm which has tended finally to undermine itself so that we have today reached a "point of convergence"—clearly then a post-modern phase—a situation which in one aspect is one of emptiness and gratuity opening up untrammeled creativity, or in another aspect one of access to an archaic wisdom of origins again become available.

So far as actual periodization is involved, Paz writes: "What is in question in the second half of our century is not the idea of art itself but the idea of the modern." Our own present marks the end of the avant-garde and of the period dating from the eighteenth century of modern art. Today, instead of the accelerating succession of innovations with its formula of "tradition versus the new," we have a situation in which the new moment is not "new" but "other." We have an "aesthetic of surprise." "All time and space flow together in one here and now." The avant-garde had continued the revolt of modernism but with more violence so that the limits of art had been reached. Thus today we see the fragmentation of the avant-garde, the confusion of genres, the undermining of the idea of the work of art. Thus the way has been opened to recovery of the object not as something to be possessed but as a presence to be contemplated.

The end of modernism is here viewed above all as the end of an alienating rationalism. But in this context rationalism is identified with all Western humanism: not only the Age of Reason but Romanticism, not only Judeo-Christian asceticism but also classical dualism. The upshot is clearest at two points. (1) We are entering *Another Time:* "neither linear or cyclical; neither history or myth . . . a carnal, a mortal time." (2) The new time is especially identified as that of *the erotic.* This means a negation of all Western versions of "nonbody" whether religious or atheist, philosophical or political, materialist or idealist. It is a time of "the return of the presence of the beloved."

Much of *Conjunctions and Disjunctions* reflects a widely recognized insistence that the modern consciousness unmask and explore the elemental realities of the body and its wisdom, the dynamics and symbolics of the carnal. Paz's discussion deals with sexual symbol in East and West, in art and liturgy, and the antinomies of love and excrement, ass and face, pleasure principle and death.

The findings of this intercultural survey are linked in the later book with a predictable critique of the Calvinist ethic which is seen— because of its pragmatic futurism—as responsible for a devaluation of the present, but also for the deconsecration of the body in capitalism: the garden of delights becomes only a rationalized tool.

> Nowadays the rebellion of the body is also that of the imagination. Both reject linear time; their values are those of the present . . . the images of desire dissolve past and future into a timeless present. It is the return of the beginning of the beginning, to the sensibility and passion of the Romantics. The resurrection of the body may be an omen that man may well recover his lost wisdom. (p. 156f.)

Or as he writes in the earlier book, the word *presence* and the word *love* "were the seed of the West, the origin of our art and poetry. In them is the secret of our resurrection" (p. 139).

It is evident that post-modern reality for Paz means a radical break with the *ratio* and ethos of the whole humanist tradition. If we ask for a grammar of meaning or even of an aesthetic in connection with the wisdom of "presence" or "festival" or "love" we shall be accused of outworn syndromes. That point of convergence now open to us, that wisdom or *arche* which can be repristinated, may, indeed, be understood in categories familiar to us as a recovery of the sense of wonder and of elemental impulse. But Paz means more than this. As his whole discussion makes clear, a special ontology is in view.

The meaning of "love" has far other implications than the *eros* which Paz evidently intends by it. "Love in the Western world," as de Rougemont and others have explored it, has had various transformations and antecedents. But in the main tradition the structures of love presuppose—even ontologically—a "world" in some sense personal, temporal, indeed historical. This is an order of reality which "the passion of the Romantics," and the timeless images of desire, and the buried arcana of the soul, Eastern and Western, have always sought to escape. Any resurrection of the West apart from this realm of meaning can only represent an impoverishment of the human.

For my purpose the most immediate query relates to the simplification here in the view of modernism. Paz follows what I would see as only one of its trajectories or veins, that rigorously iconoclastic impulse which moves only toward dissolution and to a negation, which is also an old and a new wisdom, actually a turn toward an Other, a probe of the chthonic or abyssal. But there have been other trajectories in modernism which while being iconoclastic have also been transformative of the tradition. In many artists and on many fronts the modern imagination has exhibited wrestlings with the epochal disorder and with the erosion of its language and symbolics. Thus continuities of meaning and indeed public, even political, meaning have been maintained as against that increasing unreality and loss of norm so widely hailed.

But this leads to the deeper query. In his book on Lévi-Strauss[9] Octavio Paz returns persistently to the problem of the meaning of meaning. He recognizes the fateful dominance of subjectivity and psychologism in our period, the exaggeration of the subject after Descartes. As Susan Sontag has stated it: "the modern man lives with an increasing burden of subjectivity at the expense of his sense of the reality of the world."[10] But Paz sees this erosion again as a salutary disenchantment with our Western sense of reality. Our task is knowledge of the void. As one commentator on Paz writes, all artistic activity toward the end of our century has the character of a meditation on the vertigo of nonbeing.

9. *Claude Lévi-Strauss: An Introduction* (Ithaca and London: 1970).
10. *Against Interpretation* (New York: 1966), 134.

Thus in our age of *transplantés linguistiques* we are beyond the epoch in which substantial aspects of reality could be invoked by "correspondences" (Baudelaire), by nostalgias or myths, or by surrealism. Paz discusses the cases of Sartre and Lévi-Strauss. Nihilism for Sartre was historicist and could only be overcome by his own special and arbitrary version of transcendence. Sartre was a thinker of the first half of our century. Nihilism for Lévi-Strauss is identified with a prehistorical materialism. But as a thinker of the second part of the century, for him "matter is not a substance but a relation." Lévi-Strauss seeks an analogue of rationality here. Citing Ricoeur, Paz notes that this "materialism" has its quasi-Platonic categories. In the autonomous manifestations of this alien order in human consciousness and fabulation Paz sees a kinship with Buddhism which he thinks is not accidental. "It is one more proof that the West, by its own means, and by the very logic of its history, is now arriving at conclusions fundamentally identical with those Buddha and his disciples had arrived at."

But again I note that Paz in his phrase, "by the very logic of its history," is referring to that particular trajectory of modernism which he chooses to preempt as central. I must object again, however, that there has been much in modernism which has been antimodernist in the sense Paz assigns to it. That course toward nihilism and that loss of the sense of the reality of the world which he identifies have, indeed, had their occasions in the intellectual and cultural life of certain strata of our period, but differing options and interpretations have all along been represented. It is particularly in their *cleavage* from the vitalities and sense of continuity of the anonymous multitudes that the intelligentsia and the elites have forfeited nourishment. But contrariwise it is thanks to these that ancient orders of life and survival, ritual moral and religious, have their fertility. Those who have spoken for them in depth, a Faulkner, a Brecht, a David Jones, an Auden, have included the task of dismantling in that of a larger affirmation. In particular they have escaped the solipsism or pseudomysticisms of the age by their transformations of the political imagination of the past.

Octavio Paz's post-modern view of our situation in terms of convergence has special authority for us as coming from a Spengler-like polymath, initiate into many cultures, East and West, as well as a representative of the Third World. In concluding, however, as he does that we are back at the beginning of the beginning, and that the word *presence* and the word *love* were the seeds of the West, and that in them is the secret of our resurrection and of our lost wisdom, many of us cannot but be puzzled. Despite the prodigious sophistication we seem to have heard this before, whether from a long line of antinomians, nativists, organicists, apostles of spontaneity or even the flower children.

R. Poggioli ends his book *The Theory of the Avant-Garde* (1968) on a somewhat similar note. "The avant-garde is the extreme anticlassical reaction of the modern spirit . . . but also a revolution. . . . The fourth phase, which is one of rest and readjustment may also be the moment of realization and conquest . . . a tendency destined to become art in spite of itself or even in the out-and-out denial of itself" (p. 231). In closing he cites Apollinaire as one speaking for this promise.

Nous ne sommes pas vos ennemis
Nous voulons vous donner de vastes et d'étranges domaines
Ou le mystère en fleurs s'offre à qui veut le cueillir.

In all such cases we have learned to suspect "myths of innocence" which take us back to that Garden and to those vitalities which the whole human story has taught us the need of ordering. Moreover, in decreating our historic cultures, unless we sift and select, we forfeit the warp and woof of our most precious human reality and its imaginative and affective registers.

V

For us in the West the chief debate and unfinished business has to do with our Hebraic rather than our Greek antecedents since our understanding of time and our archetypes of social order derive so largely from the former. The modern spirit has been restive with these biblical patterns and their perversions, and convulsive assertions of autonomy have sought to throw off the whole incubus of history. So we would exchange the *humanum* for the *novum*, legislate the Year One or the intemporal for the calendar, and escape the torments of freedom and conscience by a plunge into the arcane. But as W.H. Auden, the cartographer of the modern, so often urged, to return to the Garden of spontaneity is only to find ourselves once again at the precise point at which the Hebrew experience of freedom began, that freedom whose dynamics it saved from confusion and sterility.

The erosion of the sense of reality and of meaningfulness in question actually characterizes our elites rather than our more rooted strata and communities, and our elites more often as Zeitgeist and ideology than as radical devastation. Where it is present and where it constitutes itself as a program, it must inevitably traduce the sound aspects of our culture, whether as found in the university or in religious traditions or in our social covenants. This bears especially upon any structures of moral authority, immediately identified as negative and repressive.

As suggested above, a favorite whipping boy of modernism and post-modernism has been Calvinism, especially in its Anglo-Saxon forms. Since the structures of Calvinism, as distinct even from those of Lutheranism, borrow so immediately from the Old Testament this brings us back again to the matter of our Hebraic antecedents. So far as continental iconoclasm has looked for archetypes of any kind in Western tradition it has looked to Hellas rather than to Israel. But this bypasses the deep underpinnings of Western societies represented by the biblical models. Only Marxism has been a partial exception.

As an intellectual shaped by Latin culture Octavio Paz shares this imbalance especially as it bears on an appreciation of the psychic and moral continuities in Christendom. This comes out especially in his simplistic clichés shared with French intellectuals about American society and its Calvinist temper and biblical mold. Continental sophisticates, especially the Latins, have always had a complete block in understanding Puritan and Calvinist ethos and its own kind of cultural fertility.[11]

But behind this particular issue as to Calvinism—and bearing on any diagnosis of Western Christendom—is the more general question

---

11. The special nuance of the serious, *le sérieux*, the earnest, the intransigent, in Puritan cultures, has always been incomprehensible to the Latin. (A reverse incomprehension is to be found of course in characterization of the Latin as *frivole*.) One illustration: in Paris after the Armistice when it might have been agreed that Woodrow Wilson had made some contribution to the common victory, his use of prayer before a public ceremony was greeted with hilarity by the French press.

as to the Hebraic matrices. Whether for good or ill our surviving sense as to the coherence of things and of time's successions, together with the cement of our polities and social forms, traces in large part to these ancient annals of world-making. Revolt against these constellations in our unconscious—as in the case of the Nazi mania—can only lead into alienation, a forfeiture of substance and meaning. As in earlier epochs decreation or linguistic change should go hand in hand with repossession.

Unfortunately our higher culture perpetuates misconceived and negative views of the Hebrew Scriptures themselves. A supposedly sophisticated disesteem of these as entailing judgmentalism and psychic guilt, aggression and violence, upon later generations of three world faiths, a view one finds reechoed in many contexts, rests in part on inadequate literary reading of the texts, in part on a strong strain of eudaemonism which shrinks at too much of reality. Israel's charters evoke a theater of existence with whose dynamics and orders humanism has always found it difficult to come to terms.

The savage vendettas and bans of extermination in the Hebrew annals should be read not only in the light of their times but also with due recognition of those oral and literary genres which are their vehicles. The austere oracles of the prophets should be read in the light of those dynamics of existence which other cultures have assigned to Shiva the Destroyer, to the Thracian Dionysos or to those emblems of the devouring abyss found in pre-Columbian art.[12]

It would be unjust to characterize the kind of cultural scanning of the West represented by Paz and many others as only aesthetic or hedonist. But it misreads the Hebraic quotient in our societies. Our intellectuals return ever and again to Hellenic premises, including those of the pre-Socratics, on their way perhaps to some deeper or

12. Robert Lowell, who lectured on the Bible as literature at Harvard, would demur understandably at the bloodbaths in the Books of Joshua and Revelation without taking account, however, as one would expect in comparative literary procedure, of the traditional rhetorical media in question. In a recent book, *Beyond*, I.A. Richards laments the pedagogical consequences through the centuries of the sanguinary elements in the ancient chronicles. But what of their ultimate nexus with the issues of chaos and order? Long ago Ezra Pound classed such savage tales of heroes and feuds in the Bible with those of the Iroquois and contrasted them with the lofty vein of Confucius and the sublimity of the God of Dante. But here surely is a confusion of contexts, not to mention the line which runs from the fateful rigor of the old folktales to the structures of the *Divine Comedy*.

more global *arche*. They are in a sense belated *Graeculi*. George
Steiner is here an exception. His Hebraic initiation makes it possible
for him to recognize in twentieth-century social psychology a convulsive wrestling with the austerities of Jewish monotheism, related to
the holocaust and to cultural anomie and guilt symptoms.

Without acclaiming the promise of a new post-modern threshold,
Steiner has made important observations as to our crisis. In his
Bluebeard's Castle: Some Notes Towards the Redefinition of Culture
(1971) he analyzes the "nostalgia for disaster" and the "aesthetics of
violence" in our century, and, as I have noted, the self-flagellation of
the West related not only to the holocaust but to revolt, public and
latent, against the demands of Jewish monotheism and early Christian rigor. With the loss of confidence in progress and the interrup-
tions of older continuities the arts move toward the happening and
"anonymous social creativity." The debilitation of literacy can hardly
be compensated for by the flourishing but abstract literacy of mathe-
matics and the sciences.

In the section on "Topologies of Culture" in *After Babel* (1976)
Steiner asks about our disarray at the level of language. "Meaning is
a function of social-historical antecedents and shared responses." Will
the "dynamic traditionality" so distinctive of Western literacy per-
sist? How deep is our cultural incoherence in view of its barbarism,
populism, technologization, trivialization? He notes that those who
gave us the "modern classics" felt themselves to be "anguished custo-
dians" of the past, and that even the more extreme strategies represented by collage "have been set against an informing background
and framework of tradition." "It may be," he concludes, "that cultural
traditions are more firmly anchored in our syntax than we realize,
and that we shall continue to translate from the past of our individual
and social being whether we would or not." In any case Steiner is no
evangelist of an emancipated post-modern creativity.

In many of these matters I find my own best guide in Frank
Kermode. In his essay "The Modern" in his *Modern Essays*,[13] while he
is ready to distinguish a "palaeo-modern" and a "neo-modern," he
finds the latter demonstrably a continuation of the former. "There
has been only one Modernist Revolution, and it happened a long

13. (London: Collins [Fontana Books], 1971), 39–70.

time ago. So far as I can see there has been little radical change in modernist thinking since then." With Leslie Fiedler in mind as its spokesman Kermode then rejects the idea that there has latterly been a "mutation"—social and aesthetic—in our situation, involving some kind of breakthrough "into new psychic possibilities."

Kermode's discussion is based on cases drawn not only from literature but from painting and music.[14] He grants that moral and spiritual judgments, whether neo-modern life-style and art are dangerous or not, are "not in his brief." But he is evidently concerned with the continuities of cultural and linguistic meaning.

> It is now fashionable to regard our plight as without parallel, and the past as irrelevant—an . . . error, and one which is responsible for further ideological muddle, as well as for a certain false opposition between palaeo- and neo-modernism. Nothing can so muddle argument as the claim that there exist no standards by which an argument can be judged, or even no language in which it can be opposed.[15]

The problem of "naming the real" in our epoch has no doubt imposed an enormous task on the modern poet and artist. Their language-trouvailles and what Pound called trying and prying and stretching and tampering with the media have been paralleled at the discursive level in philosophy, social science and criticism. In this wide engagement with a changing climate it is not surprising that our mages and augurs have probed and scanned new realities, even the most arcane. In such conjunctions where continuities are themselves obscure it is difficult to know whether, in Kermode's phrase, one is retrieving or abolishing tradition. Loss of substance is all the more likely because artist and school become absorbed in new strategies rather than in the prior responses. So also special sensitivities establish themselves with only a tenuous relation to any point of departure.

The issue as to "meaning" and as to the "real" is no doubt raised in its most acute form by those who acclaim a post-modern situation, a mutation in consciousness and the arts, another reality to be explored apart from the ancient habits in which at least Western man

---

14. One example, "Aleation in the arts, I suggested, pushed into absurdity a theory based on observation, that chance or grace plays a role in composition" (p. 56). "Aleatory art is accordingly, for all its novelty, an extension of past art, indeed the hypertrophy of one aspect of that art" (p. 58).

15. Ibid., p. 47.

has oriented himself in time, nature and polity. Whether such openness is envisaged as total or as a return to archaic "seeds of wisdom," whether it is evoked by shamanism or by a fertile emptiness or by the analogy of play, whether it is set against a screen of nihilism or some occult mythology of gnosticism, the final test remains. The final question as to any representation, fantasy, graph, emblem, rune or utterance is that of *reference*, referentiality, the ground of communication. But this test which older epochs have called "truth" would set in motion again all the tropisms, all the impulses toward coherence and survival, of the species from the beginning, moral and cognitive as well as imaginative.

So far as our modernisms have identified new antennae for the exploration of the psyche and the world, or liberated some pristine sensorium of our being from overlays of social habit, the gains and strategies should be prized, but incorporated into older wisdoms. But I recall here the caution of Adolf Portmann cited earlier: our human stock has its millennially inbuilt givens and human culture its ancient determinations. Within certain limits, variations, novelties, mutants, are nourished by the inherited plasma or codes. Outside those limits the mutant is the monstrous.

Index